. . . AGAIN

ALSO BY MARK NOWAK

Social Poetics
Coal Mountain Elementary
Shut Up Shut Down
Revenants

. . . AGAIN

Mark Nowak

Minneapolis
2026

Cover design by Carlos Esparza
Book design by Mark Nowak

Coffee House Press books are available to the trade through our primary distributor, Consortium Book Sales & Distribution, cbsd.com or (800) 283-3572. For personal orders, catalogs, or other information, write to info@coffeehousepress.org.

Coffee House Press is a nonprofit literary publishing house. Support from private foundations, corporate giving programs, government programs, and generous individuals helps make the publication of our books possible. We gratefully acknowledge their support in detail in the back of this book.

LIBRARY OF CONGRESS CATALOGING-IN-PUBLICATION DATA

Names: Nowak, Mark, 1964- author
Title: . . . AGAIN / Mark Nowak.
Description: Minneapolis : Coffee House Press, 2026.
Identifiers: LCCN 2025044531 (print) | LCCN 2025044532 (ebook) | ISBN 9781566897518 paperback | ISBN 9781566897525 epub
Subjects: LCGFT: Abecedariuses
Classification: LCC PS3614.O96 A33 2026 (print) | LCC PS3614.O96 (ebook)
LC record available at https://lccn.loc.gov/2025044531
LC ebook record available at https://lccn.loc.gov/2025044532

PRINTED IN THE UNITED STATES OF AMERICA

33 32 31 30 29 28 27 26   1 2 3 4 5 6 7 8

TABLE OF CONTENTS

FALL [1]

WINTER [31]

SPRING [61]

SUMMER [91]

FALL (. . . AGAIN) [121]

*

Notes & Acknowledgements [175]

. . . AGAIN

DOLLAR TREE
PIZZERIA
LIQUORS
TRUMP
2020

FALL

Not another anthem but another anathema. Another antigen. The bottles of Aleve at Family Dollar are identical to the bottles of Aleve at Dollar Tree. It's that time of the year. Late autumn. Joint pain, muscle pain, Joint Chiefs of Staff. Attorney General, Surgeon General, Dollar General. Not another anthem but another rant at 'em. Another *chanson.* Buy the Dawn's early grease cutting action. Autumn air, fallen leaves. Arby's parking lot, snowplow markers already anchored in the nearly frozen mud. Not another anthem but another manthem, another Ku Klux Klanthem. American-made (union-made) pickup trucks flying Confederate flags in northern New York. Autumn, fall, days and days of cascading leaves. Not another anthem but another gun-toting Karenthem, another Mitch McCanthem, another Steve Bannonthem. Just can't, them. Fox News on wide screens seen from the rural roadsides after dark. Another year older, another year whiter. Wiser? Pfizer. Another anthem, another tantrum. Another fake news phantom.

Breaking news. Bodies broke and broken. Abandoned factories and farm machinery. Ancient breaking-down biospheres, fractured bones. Big Lots parking lot next to the blood bank. Medical beds. Bodies beneath white sheets. Refrigerator trucks behind hospitals. Listen to the bellowing voices. Balderdash. Been here before yet never been here before. Black cloth masks, black surgical masks, black KN95 masks, black N95 masks: a materialist history. Autobody shops and Burger Kings. Don't be bashful. Become more boisterous and boastful like the old boys of before. Just don't be a bystander. Be a braggart. Like beer. Be a bulldozer. Because the flags are out. Trump 2020 flags, Fuck Biden flags ripping in the blustery winds, hay bales covered in frost. Brutal times. But maybe at least there will be Big Macs and reruns of *Breaking Bad* again. Banana Republics by-and-by. Less baggage. Baby Gaps in a reopened mall. It's not so much the end that scares us as it is the beginning of the end. Bear markets. Boom and bust. Buyer beware.

Covered this before: wagons, bridges, cracks in the concrete. A late lunch at Cracker Barrel maybe, then swing by Costco. The climate of the country is cheap, or maybe that's its character. Checkered past. Checkered future. But a colossal war chest. Counting down the hours until dusk. Trump tests positive for Covid, flies in a helicopter to Walter Reed National Military Medical Center, is driven around in a heavily modified Chevrolet Suburban as he waves at the cameras and the crowds. It's callous and it's contagious. The skies are partly cloudy. But at what cost? A collapsing economic infrastructure. Cardboard cutouts at a rifle range. Conspiracy theories. The die have been cast. Golden Corral and Colonie Diner and Tex's Chicken & Burgers all on the same block of Central Avenue. It's a conundrum. Calculating the clearance sales, getting used to the everything must go's. Abandonment in Buffalo and at the Berkshire Mall. Nothing now but carryout, Chick-fil-As and Chipotles. OKCupid. It's common sense for the culprits. For capitalism. Closing time. Take care, cousins. Take care, comrades. To be discontinued. Be still my beating corpse.

Dumpster dives, damaged goods, debris. Yet there's almost always a family of deer at dusk out behind the Family Dollar. In the deciduous trees beyond the loading dock. The sun still goes down, daily, behind the mountains on the other side of these beige cinder block walls if you're here at this darkening hour. Maybe America is dying. The devil's in the details. Covid-19. Frontline workers at a booth at Denny's, in the drive-thru at Dunkin' and the DQ. Never mind the deindustrialization. Never mind the demons, the doomsdays, the drugs. The dead have forever been the about to be dying, and days before that they were at the dentist's office or shopping at Dress Barn. Or maybe shopping for Dr Pepper at Dollar General or Mountain Dew at Dollar Tree. Remember when Trump bought the Clemson football team McDonald's, Wendy's, Burger King, and Domino's? We're told it's anti-democratic to criticize capitalism. To think about everyday life in detention camps, the daily dropping of drone bombs. Dudes. This is what democracy has looked like since democracy was born. Deal with it. Depart or deport.

Encyclopedias and empires go extinct. Eternity isn't an option. Enjoy the evanescent moon before it evaporates into another eerie dawn, eerie day. Shuttered used car lot across the street from Wastequip headquarters sells eggs for $3 a dozen and flies a Blue Lives Matter flag. It's the ecosystem nowadays. The Anthropocene. Chickens coming home to roast. The rent is overdue. Eventually we won't be hired any more, won't be here anymore. It happened at the Energizer battery factory in Burlington, Vermont. Imagine the Energizer Bunny with no more *joie de vivre*. "We are committed to making our colleagues' transition(s) as smooth as possible." So start searching for jobs on Indeed. Please. It's always been about entropy. At either end of Lake Erie, the abandoned factories: Buffalo, Cleveland, Toledo, Detroit (though a few factories have been gentrified into condos for the elites). Drive through Albany and head east. Drive from Pittsfield to North Adams to the Vermont border. Endless empty parking lots, endless erosion. It isn't erroneous to think this way. It's the essence of this country. The evacuations will be everlasting.

Fox News. Fake news. Early onset fascism. Combine harvesters covered in faux camouflage plastic tarps. Covered in freezing rain or frost. The fields lie fallow for now. From small fissures to earthquake fault lines. Somewhere flapjacks must be burning. Fire alarms going off. History isn't usually written by the forgotten. Frontline workers. Foodtown cashiers. What's forsaken is forsaken. And it's already being forgotten. Yet every year there's this magnificent autumn around here. Red and orange leaves falling into the culverts, up on the roof of the chicken farmer's farmhouse, in soon-to-be blown away arrangements. Photograph them with your iPhone. Flotsam for the owners. Jetsam for the workers. Funeral music. More flags flying at half-mast. Anthony Fauci. All that ferocity and filth. All that fog. Fuck it, let's drive down to Five Guys. And afterwards, let's head over to Family Dollar and grab some Fritos and Double Stuf Oreos. It's fascinating to see it all aflame. It's a full moon, Hunter's moon. What's forthcoming is forthcoming if we can get there from here. Freight trains rumbling through the darkness. "Never forget."

Gasps of cold wind, gathering clouds. A pack of Goldfish cheddar crackers from Dollar General we eat in the parking lot of Bill's Top of the Hill Citgo. Trump 2020 bumper stickers on the SUVs coming to get gas. Get out or get ready to get out. It's a given. Like some modern version of Golgotha or Gethsemane. Like some burial ground for all these Covid corpses. Grasping when we aren't gasping. Governing yet ungovernable. But I digress. An Army-green 5-gallon plastic gasoline can getting filled for the long winter ahead. Glamour Nails, Glamour Shots, all the shuttered stores. Housatonic Street at Hot Dog Ranch. Guns in the racks of the American-made pickup trucks. G-strings you get from Amazing Intimates & Smoke. We're going where we're going, America. Sometimes gaudy, sometimes gangrene. So down another Yuengling. Drink another Genesee Cream Ale. The ghosts among us are no longer genuflecting. Goldenrod, Canadian geese waving goodbye with their wings. You could go against the grain, but the windows of The Gap were covered with plywood long ago. The next generation just goes to Google. Give in already or go down in flames.

Heaven isn't happening here again. Just hover over the abandoned factory landscapes with a drone. See the heretics, the hypocrites, the laughing hyenas. It's our heritage. Hello, abandoned warehouses. Hello, small houses losing a few shingles each fall. It's hellish. And so much heroin. The darkening days just before and after Halloween. Empty bag of Chester's Flamin' Hot Fries. Hormel Pepperoni Snack Stix. Heath bar. Hershey's Kiss. A history without history. Another history full of hand grenades. Hello, broken marriages. Hello, broken windows, broken heat pumps, broken cheekbones. Hello, rusting steel and stolen land. High above us hang white clouds and their gray shadows. Red-tailed hawk. Hi, it's me or what used to be me. A holograph of me. Everybody here is broken-hearted. We used to go to Harvey's hamburgers in southern Ontario but now we can't even cross the border to Montréal. Maybe it's Hardee's for our hangovers now. Maybe it's *Hunger Games* and Hungry-Man dinners (Salisbury steak, beer-battered chicken). The keyword here is battered. The pronouns are almost always he and him.

A white KIA / on the side of the highway / inclement weather / interrogation / ICE agents / Historics / of mass incarcerations / of mass demonstrations / of mass liquidations / You can see / the IHOP sign / from here / the IKEA billboard / In-N-Out Burger / from here / Intensive care units / intensification / of Covid-19 cases / high blood pressure / diabetes / A country / incontinent / Intravenous / injections / Infantilized / by its infantry / by its infancy / by its illegitimacy / I drive / along / the Housatonic River / as it crosses / under Route 20 / three times / Stop / sometimes / to listen to the river / water / PCBs / from the abandoned / General Electric factory / now / a Superfund site / Intolerable / and inevitable / Cinder block architecture / Family Dollar / Dollar General / Bioaccumulation / in the birds / Red-winged blackbirds / white-throated sparrows / blue jays and brown-headed cowbirds / Night is / up against / whatever makes / the owls / so seldom / afraid / of the night / Goodwill store / abandoned / its windows / dirty / FOR LEASE sign / in blood-red letters / the asphalt / in the parking lot / a sheet of / early / ice.

It's just another empty parking lot outside another shuttered JCPenney. J.Crew relocated to the outlet mall outside of Lee. Need a job application? Either you're in jeopardy or you're on your couch watching *Jeopardy!* Eating Jolly Ranchers. Eating Junior Mints. Junk bonds, junkies, American jobs. So just keep a journal. Do a jigsaw puzzle. Watch just one more episode of *Hoarders*. Jack pines. Junk food. 1-800-GOT-JUNK. Jack-o'-lanterns starting to rot. Maybe look for Jupiter in the night sky. Watch reruns of *The Jetsons* or John-Boy Walton on YouTube. Jet streams. Jewelry boxes full of stars. Adjust the northern nights. Or maybe we're just in a new kind of jail. *Spiral Jetty.* Injustice and joblessness. Circle Jerks. It's in the daily newspapers behind the paywalls. Frozen Junior's cheesecake on sale at Price Chopper. Or drive to Jack in the Box and come home if you have one. Watch the killjoys on a giant flatscreen. Juxtapositions, juvenilia, juntas. Trump, at the podium, jitters and jives. Jehovah and Jekyll in one. Long live Jackie O. White jellybeans. *The New Jim Crow.* It's beginning to sound a lot like jackhammers. Every day is Judgment Day. No justice, just the police. Just junkyards. Just the braying of the jackals.

Halcyon days, like the Keynesian days, are history now. In America, there is no again. Maybe it's karma for how the country started. Knights of Columbus. KKK. Fake kink. Kmart collapsed, but the KISS Army survives. So maybe a quick trip to Kwik Trip for a Twix, or KFC for a KFC bucket because why not, the kingdom may be crumbling but at least the drive-thru is still open late. Or swing the kettlebells. Make a kale Caesar. Kill or keep track of your kilocalories. Drop another kilo. Out in the country where the kindling is kept. And kegs of kerosene. Sing karaoke. Maybe something by the Kinks or Killing Joke. Kneel with a knife over a deer carcass. Knick knack paddy whack. Pass the ketchup packets, the Chick-fil-A Zesty Buffalo sauce. Kumquats. It's just a joke. But we're not really joking anymore. Knowledge is kryptonite. The men in their beloved khakis, white knights kvetching about "urban crime." Kidnap the curriculum. Run it through the kangaroo courts. Clarence Thomas, Brett Kavanaugh, Amy Coney Barrett. Sing "Kumbaya." It's all off-kilter. It's more than a kerfuffle. Killing time sometimes. The rest is kaput.

Essential workers, frontline workers. Abandoned NAPA Auto Parts store near Lebanon Valley Speedway. Old RVs settled in for the upcoming winter. Lithium. Lingerie. A few leftover fires. Limp tires, retreads. Get Little Caesars delivered. Like it or not. Landscaping businesses. Northern lights. At one point in history we were called the lumpenproletariat (from the German *lumpen*, "rag, rogue"). Just labor now. Belabored. Refugee workers, migrant child laborers. Crumbling factories that lack capital. Lack love. An era that's lost its luster. Laughing gas, generic laundry detergent at the local laundromat. Like Gain, again. Laughingstocks. A life sentence? Every sentence feels like a lifetime ago. Lapsed payments. Lease expired. Lifetime Channel movies to help you forget. The lightbulbs are lukewarm at best. Life cycles on life support. A line of nine harvest green John Deere tractors most likely won't be sold until next spring. Lines through the parking lot at Long John Silver's. When I left this morning for a Target pickup my daughter's window shade was drawn, but when I return a few hours later her window is open to the light. If only history could be a little more like this. Haybales lightly dusted in snow. Dusky late fall sky. Foliage on the forest floor. A pair of northern cardinals singing the old lullabies.

Munchkins from the Dunkin' drive-thru at the edge of Pontoosuc Lake. A sord of mallards muck about on the soon-to-be frozen water. My Family Assault Weapons sticker on the back window of the SUV in front of me. A Blue Lives Matter sticker, too. Largemouth Bass, Smallmouth Bass, Tiger Muskellunge. Ice fishing shacks and snowmobiles coming soon. America is American after all. Morning sickness, murder mysteries, melancholia. It's programmed into the algorithms. Come to Dunkin', Big Mac Meal Deal. The madding crowd seems madder than before. In the parking lot at Walmart, mercenaries wearing MAGA caps. Buying MAGA flags on Amazon.com. So much moxie. Thunderstorms. It's late autumn. In the night sky, there's a waxing moon or a waning moon. Moonshine. Maybe or maybe not. It's like a mortuary here sometimes. Sometimes it's like a morgue. Dead deer on the side of the highway. Misty late afternoons, or is that fog again? The mountains, the coyotes in the mountains, the mice in the stomachs of the coyotes in the mountains. There's maybe a momentum here of some kind. At least we've got Munchkins and maybe we'll get a McFlurry, too. Best of times, worst of times. Pots of dying mums.

The Dollar General in Hoosick Falls, New York, is six-tenths of a mile north of Dollar Tree. Tops Friendly Markets is three-tenths of a mile north from there. That's the northern landscape nowadays. Never mind the naysayers. It's anti-American. It's in our nervous system. You're born with a choice between Takis Intense Nacho and Takis Nacho Xplosion. Now is your chance to choose. It's the beginning of November. We can't be nonchalant about it anymore. Mass shootings, Neanderthals, neophytes, some news from NASA trending on Twitter. Nix it. There's so much naked anger. So many nightmares, nervous breakdowns, night sweats, nursing home deaths. Maybe there's a new moon sometimes. Maybe an anniversary gift from Neiman Marcus or Nordstrom Rack before they shutter, too. Night stays here longer now. The night watchmen have so much more to watch. Just watch the news. It's streaming on Hulu. Nothing else is new. Even in New Amsterdam. Even in Neverland. Never say never. You never said Simon says.

Owls out in the woods behind Office Depot. The odds have been against us from the onset. Obedience, obesity, alcohol, opioids. Owls out behind Ollie's Bargain Outlet, too. Owls in the old oak trees out behind the boarded up Old Navy. Once the wind did blow through trees like these and we were here to witness them waver. Overcast clouds. Old effervescent decaying crops. October's over and so is All Hallows' Eve. Cornstalks and gourds on the ground in the dimming daylight. Maybe we're somewhere in northern Ohio or on the shores of Lake Erie or Lake Ontario or any other ordinary place where once we held each other like only we could hold each other. Sure it was ending, it would end. Sure the shopping malls would close forever. No more overtime and only so much overdraft protection. Everyone reading this now is eventually going to die. Just ask the owls, the ones in the woods out behind the abandoned Old Spaghetti Factory. We're cooked. Meth maybe. Frozen fish sticks and Banquet Turkey Pot Pies from the Dollar Tree. Vodka. OxyContin. In the pine grove out behind the shuttered Old Country Buffet. Just listen to the owls.

Pass the medium security prison and the plaza with Panera and Papa John's. Americans love a parade. A possum scurries across Route 20 and into the weeds near the pond. Puddles in the parking lots under the partially obscured moonlight. At least we used to be able to share a supper at Panda Express or P.F. Chang's. Empty Pabst Blue Ribbon and Labatt Blue cans in the parking lot after work at Wendy's. But the plazas and malls are permanently empty now. Peek inside through plate glass windows covered in butcher paper. Broken water pipes. Autumn leaves blew in when the maintenance guy propped the glass doors of JCPenney's open so he could bring in sheets of plexiglass and plywood. Old piss stains on the cracked tiles beneath the men's urinals. A porta potty left outside the abandoned Sears. Postal workers in post office trucks drive by what used to be a Pizza Hut. Ditto FedEx workers. Ditto UPS. Post some old pics on Facebook of the places and palaces of your youth. Pretend all The Pretenders survived. We have a penchant for peroxide again these days during the plague life. Politics still playing politics. A boarded up entrance to Pearle Vision. A shuttered Pepperidge Farm.

The countryside, like the country, quakes. A land of conquistadors and ventriloquists. It's quintessential, isn't it. At least it's unquestionable. Sequestered juries. Nonstop Twitter polls, questionnaires. Toxic waste in the aquifers. It's a quagmire (from quag, "a marshy place"). It's like you're in quicksand. There isn't a Quiznos or Qdoba around here anymore, but there's a Dairy Queen drive-thru in Ghent. A Walgreens for quaaludes and NyQuil. Maybe a new acquaintance who might quench your thirst trap. Or maybe it's just time to quit. Quixotic men, quotidian men. Nothing to quibble over. Prequalified homebuyers. Bad movie sequels. It's unequivocable. History has had this in the queue for centuries. Squalor, mosquitoes, pull quotes misquoted from the press. There isn't a Quick Trip anywhere around here either, but at least there's an acre of Wastequip dumpsters nearby. Honestly, it isn't very picturesque. Time to liquidate your liquid assets. It's a time of tanks and tranquilizers. Strip clubs, roadside burlesque. Land of imported tequila. Land of QAnon. We are, at best, colloquial. No question about it. No questions from the press.

A few northern flickers, a red-bellied woodpecker. An empty original Doritos bag, not that Cool Ranch kind, just the regular ones. We remember what we remember. Residue. Road rage. America is becoming more and more American. It's the routine by now, really. The egrets have migrated for the winter. We're just north of the house whose turret used to be a Tory prison. Just down the road from the graveyard where soldiers from the American Revolution have long been buried. Abandoned cinder blocks, barbed wire, three rusting Rolling Rock cans. Mud and brush sticking to my rubber boots. Another right wing Supreme Court judge. Revenge is ruthless. Dollar General announces it'll open another Dollar General between the two Family Dollars next year. A sale on Red Baron Classic Crust frozen pizza. Red-winged blackbirds in the marsh behind the Dress Barn. Redlined neighborhoods. The long-shuttered grist mills and paper mills along Stony Kill Creek. Maybe someday a Shake Shack will replace the shuttered Radio Shack. Please retweet.

A Sears Appliance Repair van. A Target semi. Stop at the Subway at Love's Truck Stop next to Dunkin'. Empty plastic Sprite bottle in the culvert across the street by the long-shuttered Lily's Diner. It's all suppressed from the news but not from streaming serials. *Hardcore Pawn. Cheaters. Diners, Drive-Ins and Dives.* This is the future of the United States of America. Take a leave of absence if you can. Maternity or sick leave. Scarecrows. Starlings. A Massachusetts state cop flying by in the same direction. Maybe a Sbarro slice or Starbucks at the interstate stop if they'd just move in to fill this endless emptiness, this endless solitude. It'll give us options at least. It used to be like how it used to be but now it's like it never was. The sky, ok, sometimes it's sanguine but there's too many streetlamps in the oversized truck stop parking lot to see the stars. Shit, shower, sleep, stock the shelves at the Dollar Store again. So many bags of Skittles, so many bags of pretzels from Snyder's of Hanover. Grab whatever you can. Stuff it into the metal handbasket you carry up and down the aisles. It's closing soon anyways. Everything is.

Trump flags saturate the landscape. It's time. Lines of voters and pollsters at the election sites. Tucker Carlson. A bag of Twizzlers from Dollar Tree. Trump 2020 billboard outside Smitty's Pizza. Cumulus clouds at the western corners of an otherwise blue sky. Tear gas. Tonight we might be able to trace the stars and the constellations with our fingertips. It's that clear. The neighbor's dog howls again after sunset. Foxes come by and overturn the trash cans, or was it that goddamn bear yet again. Check Twitter. Check your resting heart rate. History tends to reheat the past before it repeats it. Tsk, tssk. Maybe I'll put a steak on the cast iron pan tonight. Another Twisted Iced Tea can up against the chain-link fence. No one's expecting a turnaround, tbh. Toxic masculinity, toxic Housatonic River. Metal signs, the text says "DO NOT EAT/NO COMA//Fish, Frogs, Turtles, Wood Ducks, and Mallards from this River Contaminated with PCBs." Leaning toward tomorrow is leaning out of today. Check Twitter again, again. Write a Tweet. Hit delete.

Under apple trees. Under biospheres. Under-cauterized. Underdogs. Underneath everyday life. Underneath fascists (neo-fascists, pseudo-fascists, wanna-be fascists). Under God, indivisible. U-Haul near the Soldier On Veterans Food Pantry on West Housatonic Street. Undisciplined incels. Unimaginable justice for all. Under king's orders. Underloved ex-lovers. Unleashed mercenaries. Under no circumstances. Underhanded operations. Unpardonable presidents, future presidents, ex-presidents. Unquestionably so. Unregistered rifles. Unequivocal saints. Undertakers. Unvaccinated ultimatums. Ungovernable vultures. Unwarranted words. Unexpired xenophobias. Unyielding yellow crime scene tape. Unzipped zealots until the zealots are zipped up again.

You can taste the vitriol in the air. Virtue signaling. Vocabularies parched by violence. Parched by ventilators. Fevers. Emphysema. Covid-19. We're living in a vulgar state. Unnerved by the victories. Vouchsafed. Victimhood. Vicodin. Vetted yet vulnerable. And so much vengeance. So much velocity. Vast conspiracy theories. Proud Boys and Patriot Party vows. "This election is far from over." Looking like overtime. Listen to the endless ventriloquists. Watch the endless TikTok videos. Fight the endless civil wars. We the vagabonds. Veering further and further right. Revolutions. The Book of Revelation. Seven golden candlesticks, seven seals, seven trumpets, seven plagues. It's very late in the alphabet. The voting is or isn't over. Everyone's got a fever. Everyone's living in a fervor. Strange visage. Odd veneer. Vestiges of our ugly past. Bulletproof vests. It's unavoidable. Big Gulps from 7-Eleven. The velvet touch. We'll reap what this voracious and violent country has sown. Volcanoes, vasectomies, lost virginity, lost verification codes.

Watch re-runs of *The Walking Dead* after a late shift at Wendy's or White Castle. Four or five hours until dawn. Feed the felines, give the dog some fresh water. Feeling the worse for wear. West Virginia, you know what I'm talking about. Wichita, Wyoming, Milwaukee, you know why, too. Wrong way signs beside the highway exits. Boarded up windows downtown. But at least the blood bank will open soon. Winter is always ready to return with a windstorm. Watch the Weather Channel so you know what to wear to work. Heed the early warnings. Read whatever Trump tweets. Solid waste disposal. You're either watching your weight or waiting on your customers or both. Elastic waist bands. Minimum wage. So what's your future? Waffle House or Wingstop when the next shift is over. Wall Street's decided this for you decades ago. Bees wax and wane. Infowars swell. A weak economy except for the uber-wealthy. The dog wags her tail. The cats meow. Turn down the thermostat. Who can pay for all this heat in early November. *Westron wynde when wyll thow blow . . .* Wake up and smell the coffee. Get ready for work again.

Mix the ingredients in the air around us. Trump flags, Dixie flags. Sense the exasperation. Still waiting on the Covid vax. Maybe soon we'll be extinct like *Tyrannosaurus rex.* Medical examiners. Taxidermists. XY chromosomes, American exceptionalism, xenophobia. Is this the apex of November? Exhausted by the exhaust, by the intoxicated national conscience. The United States of America lacks oxygen. All we do is watch the newscasters remix the news. Exhume the bodies. Less moxie. Fewer taxis. The rich pay no taxes. Another death in Texas. This isn't a hoax. This country needs detox. Extract the prisons. Less Botox. Fewer axes to grind. Less SiriusXM Patriot and less Newsmax. Just play another song on the jukebox, baby. Expect the military jets to continue to fly over the Jets stadium. At least you can relax with football on a flatscreen, it's still late autumn after all. Expect another anthem to come next. It isn't in flux. It's the national complexion that's in crises. And that's no exaggeration. Fix it or hex it. *Vox populi.* That's the text.

Yard sales. Yellow urine stains, yellow crime scene barricade tape. Yellow HAZMAT suits. Yesterday feels like years ago. It's a Yes or No question. No answer. Yes. An empty Mickey's 40oz bottle. Yellow Butterfinger candy wrapper. It's the dying time of the sunflowers in the fields along the Amtrak tracks by Cemetery of the Maples. It's the dying time of the yellow jackets in the almost barren fields along US-90 and Stony Kill. The yellowed pages of an old Yellow Pages are history now. So many telephone numbers are dead. You may yearn for the people once attached to them, their numbers stay in your memory, yet you know in your soul where their bones have been buried, their ashes spread, their houses sold to younger homeowners who remodeled years ago. The years go by in a flash. Yes, it's more than enough of this yearning. But you can't quite seem to quit. Yes, the sun's gone down. Light the candle you bought at Yankee Candle. Drink a Mello Yello from Dollar General. Butterflies in your stomach. You only live once.

We walked toward the zenith not expecting a new rising sun. We'd be satisfied with Cheez Whiz, Zebra Cakes, and Zingers at the end of the aisle at Family Dollar. Maybe eat them with Prozac or Zoloft. Later, take in the pine trees rising behind the cinder block walls of the Dollar Tree. The American alphabet ends like every American factory ends. Zombies wandering around on Zoom. The new zoology. In the Ocean State Job Lot parking lot, I put the words "cheap America lot" into a business name generator and got Balaclava America, Zip Cheap, Burb Lot. Nothing much more needs to be said. Maybe there will be more zebras someday. More songs by the remaining members of ZZ Top (you will or will not listen to them on Bezos's Amazon Music). But for now, there are intermezzos, piazzas, and paparazzi for the elites on their mega-yachts, on their spaceship trips to outer space. Meanwhile, the working class orders a pizza delivered by the working class. Zero tolerance for everything and everyone else. Let the Dominoes fall.

TRUMP
JFK JR.Q
2020
TURN OFF THE IDIOT BOX
THEY ARE TRYING TO
DEVIDE US
THERE IS ONLY 1 RACE
THE HUMAN RACE

WINTER

All the hats are MAGA hats, that's MAGA with two As. It's agitprop, after all. Barricade fences. American Crows. Save America March. Yesterday, Trump tweeted ***Antifa is a Terrorist Organization, stay out of Washington. Law enforcement is watching you very closely.*** It's the 61st time he's tweeted about ***antifa, BLM antifa thugs, ANTIFA SCUM, ANTIFA anarchists, Antifa androgynes***, etcetera. But this morning, it's all camouflage. It's all MAGA hats. This morning it's all a sea of whiteness, an absolutely white sea. ***These people aren't going to take it any longer.*** Queen's "Bohemian Rhapsody" blares from the loudspeakers. American flags fly behind bulletproof glass. All-American, Made in America. . . . ***the China virus . . . the scam of mail-in ballots . . .*** American Barn Owls. American Psycho. Anglo Americans. American Dream. MAKE AMERICA GREAT AGAIN. A phrase as old as Ronald Reagan. ***So pure theft in American history.*** America with two As. ***Everybody knows it.*** The smoke is rising already, rising again.

And then late in the evening, or early in the morning, boom, these explosions of bullshit (the crowd chants, ***Bullshit! Bullshit! Bullshit!*** . . .). Bald eagles won't soar above these bandstands, these bystanders, these firebrands. Northern barred owls won't fly above this bacchanal. A national binge, a national bender, a debauched jamboree. Oath Keepers keep broad lists of "Orders We Will Not Obey." Just ask Joe Biggs. Ask Elmer Stewart Rhodes. Just ask the Proud Boys. ***Stand back, stand by.*** Just so many bees, swarming and stinging. Broad-winged hawks. Blockbusters. Borders. Even more barricades. ***Our country has been under siege for a long time.*** Long before today. From the beginning, tbh. So let's be honest. Blatant truths are being butchered. Everywhere America is burning. Black jackets, black boots, black SUVs, black sunglasses, black leather gloves. ***. . . a communist country . . . a bad story . . . the hoaxes and the lies that we've been forced to believe.*** A barrage of true believers who've been planning to barge in, barrel in. Babies, bitterly born. Believe me.

Carrion birds. Cantankerous crowds. Overcast skies concerned with what's beneath them. A citadel. A circus. An ocean of flags and camouflage. A white sea. A cold and brackish pond at least. A swamp for sure. ***But now, the caravans . . . the caravans are forming again.*** Build a wall. Construct a new narrative, a more contemporary conclusion. Collision? Collusion? . . . ***this enormous crowd . . . this great country . . .*** Khaki and blaze orange the colors of this conflagration. *Don't Tread on Me* flags, caustic and coiled. Fire-engine red MAGA caps. ***And if you don't fight like hell, you're not going to have a country anymore.*** Cold cases. Collateral damage. A colossal carnival. The commons vs. the commoners. Clearinghouses, House of Representatives. Distant slaughterhouse workers forced to work through Covid-19. Cajoling cliques. Mobs coalescing. Clementine-colored hair. ***So we're going to, we're going to walk down Pennsylvania Avenue. I love Pennsylvania Avenue. And we're going to the Capitol . . .*** Cooper's hawk, more crows. *Here ye, here ye,* the town crier cries out to his acolytes. . . . ***to the Capitol . . .*** Come one, come all. From the loudspeakers, Elton John's "Tiny Dancer." From the loudspeakers, Village People's "Y.M.C.A."

Down Madison Avenue, down Constitution Drive, down Independence Ave NW. Domino's delivery directions or *coup d'état*. Doesn't matter. Just don't doubt the doomsday scenarios. The doublespeak. The Dow Jones Industrial Average. The national debt. Walk by *My God! What Is This?* historical marker, the spot where Charles Guiteau shot President Garfield. Twice. Garfield died in the oceanside town of Elberon, New Jersey (4 miles north of Asbury Park). But duh, that's history now. Everything's a streamed series on the History Channel. Just walk past Frederick Law Olmsted's Summerhouse and dream about the daffodils. See the daguerreotypes, the documentaries about our deadlier moments. Jeffrey Dahmer. The Branch Davidians. Covid-19. Death is our most perfected form of democracy. It's midday now. Drones drone overhead. Walk by Tony Smith's sculpture, *The Snake is Out*. Mad hatters in red MAGA hats. Dark serpents, double-dealers, Judas Iscariots right here in the flesh. District of Columbia. The dustheaps of history. Dumpster fires. American junkyards, American graveyards. But I digress.

The Ellipse is empty. Everybody's marching to save America. A white man in a red MAGA hat rips away the plastic fencing near the Capitol Reflecting Pool. It's barely a barricade, tbh. Snow fencing essentially. So excited, so effusive, white flagpole bearers, red MAGA hat wearers. Everyday white Americans marching past the Peace Monument, flying their favorite flags alongside the Ulysses S. Grant Memorial. Entering the alabaster steps of the United States Capitol. Shouting at a few cops in blue or black surgical masks, none in riot gear. Have not seen bald eagles here. Eastern screech owls either. Just this white eclipse. "AREA CLOSED" signs hang on metal fences that don't seem to matter to the *Don't Tread on Me* men. Everywhere there are fires we won't be able to extinguish. They're effervescent now, omnipresent now. Effigies singing elegies. And even more flags, even more camouflage. Streams upon streams of pepper spray. Enter the effluvium. Enter at your own risk. There's no exit here. Just these great white neighbors sailing upon these great white seas. A great white siege. Everybody knows it.

Flag, Appeal to Heaven (aka, tree flag) ::: Flag, A.F. ("America First") ::: Flag, America First for Trump ::: Flag, Arizona (state) ::: Flag, Arizona for Trump ::: Flag, The Battle Cry (gold lamé, Joshua 6:12) ::: Flag, Betsy Ross ::: Flag, Blue Lives Matter ::: Flag, Blue Trump ::: Flag, California (state) ::: Flag, Calvin Peeing on Biden ::: Flag, Canada ::: Flag, "Come and Take It" ::: Flag, Confederate ::: Flag, Connecticut (state) ::: Flag, Cuba ::: Flag, Culpeper Minutemen ::: Flag, Don't Tread On Me (Gadsden flag) ::: Flag, Florida for Trump ::: Flag, 45 ::: Flag, Fuck Biden ::: Flag, Georgia (state) ::: Flag, Gun Owners for Trump ::: Flag, Hybrid half-U.S.A., half-Confederate ::: Flag, Ichthys (aka, Christian Jesus Fish) ::: Flag, Keep America Great ::: Flag, Kekistan (based on Nazi Swastika) ::: Flag, India ::: Flag, Infowars.com ::: Flag, Israel ::: Flag, LGBTQ+ Rainbow ::: Flag, Maryland (state) ::: Flag, Moultrie (Liberty/Quarter Moon) ::: Flag, North Carolina (state) ::: Flag, No Socialism ::: Flag, Oath Keepers ::: Flag, Old Glory ::: Flag, POW-MIA ::: Flag, Presidential Seal ::: Flag, Q (QAnon) ::: Flag, Red Trump ::: Flag, Republic of Georgia ::: Flag, Skull & Crossbones ::: Flag, SoCal Trump ::: Flag, South Carolina Navy Ensign ::: Flag, South Korea ::: Flag, South Vietnam ::: Flag, "Stop the Steal" ::: Flag, Texas (state) ::: Flag, Texas "Come and Get It" (with assault rifle on top) ::: Flag, Thin Blue Line (Maine) ::: Flag, Three Percenters ::: Flag, Tongo ::: Flag, Trump/Pence ::: Flag, Trump Rambo ::: Flag, Trump Superimposed over Gadsden Flag ::: Flag, 2020 No More Bullshit ::: Flag, 28th Virginia Battle ::: Flags, unidentified ::: Flag, Unleash the Kraken ::: Flag, Upside-down American ::: Flag, U.S.A. ::: Flag, Women for Trump ::: Flag, VDARE Lion ::: Flag ::: Flag :::

:::

:::

:::

:::

:::

:::

:::

:::

:::

:::

:::

:::

:::

:::

:::

:::

:::

:::

:::

:::

:::

:::

:::

Gates break. Great neighbors break certain fences when they want. Police barricades, bike racks, galvanized chain-link fence. Gates at which these neighbors gnaw and gnarl. Many wearing baseball caps, Trump ones, MAGA ones, American flag hats. Old glory. Once upon a time is generally once upon a time. Picture garrisons, gizzards, bludgeonings, guillotines. It's ghastly out here. It's grotesque. All these great white neighbors, like the great white ghosts gone before them, the ancestor kind, their kin. Most given male genitalia by their God, tbh. They see a gap between the gates and gatekeepers whose Blue Lives so so mattered to these once great neighbors whose blue flags they once flew from their porches and American-made pickups. *Trump 2020 Fuck Your Feelings* flag flies right in the face of a cop. Goading them on. No great horned or great grey owls here. No guardian angels or guard dogs. Just landed gentry, goatees, gristle, guts. There's going to be a gulag. No guidance. No grace. Just the great white neighbors gorging on their greatness again.

Heaven isn't here. It's a haven for heathens. Hooligans. Headlines. A Trump flag hangs over some white hero's shoulders. ***Whose house? Our house!*** Hatchet men, hangmen, former Army infantry men. ***Do you want your house back? Take it!*** A white knight robed in a Gadsden rattlesnake flag. ***We are taking our house!*** Here are your harbingers of hate. Here, hysteria and hallucinations. Herd immunity overwhelmed by herd mentality. ***We Love Trump! We Love Trump! We Love Trump!*** Someone hollering his hallelujahs in the scrum. Hecklers. Howlers. Hoots. White buildings above white marble stairs, white columns. The White House. The white seas of this white siege. White silhouettes everywhere, most in red MAGA hats or Proud Boys orange knit winter caps. Honestly, if you wear a black hoodie with white letters that says *ENRIQUE TARRIO / DID NOTHING / WRONG,* well hey, what more do I really have to say here. Cut to the handshakes and headsets. A real American hullabaloo. Iron heels. Hamsters on a wheel. Cut to the heartbreak, the hand grenades. On the horizon, hurricanes loom.

Insisting the election is illegitimate doesn't make it so. Disinformation campaigns. Social distortion. It's insipid. Live streamers like Anthime Gionet, aka, "Baked Alaska." It isn't infrequent. It's winter this mid-afternoon but there aren't any icicles. The moon is in its waxing gibbous phase. January sixth. Trees across the US Capitol grounds disinherited their leaves months ago. A dusky ivory sky whispers or whimpers through their limbs. Everything feels inauthentic even with ice storms in AccuWeather's ten-day forecast. Surveillance culture. C-SPAN's live feed. Twitter videos. We're all watching America becoming inflamed yet again. Legions of lies. Welcome to the panopticon. A white man in aviator goggles. ***Let's get their guns! Let's get their guns!*** He isn't being ironic. It's embedded in his imagination. It's all over the breaking news. *Insurgent*, from the late Latin *insurgere*, "rise up, gather force." It's incommensurable. Inaudible. Ignition sequence. *Trump 2020 Keep America Great!* banner, tied to a metal frame, is hoisted through the crowd like a coffin.

Just the first wave. Just thousands of great neighbors. Just a jaunt in the park. Or a junta. Black crows nearby. American crows. Just so much cawing. Maybe the certification of the election is about to begin. These swarms of great neighbors know the injustice. They're just so juiced. Everybody's so jovial. It's their job to keep the doors ajar. It's their job to go for the jugular. Jake Angeli. Court jesters. Just jonesing here. Juking. Like in the Book of Job. Like Jim Jones. Like Alex Jones. Just so much camouflage. Just so many MAGA hats. Jackknifing themselves past all the window frames and doorjambs. Just the second wave. Just the sixth day of the new year. Just white seas upon white seas of white men. Just swamps of them, heaps of them. Like someone just opened a jar full of jackals. A jar full of juggernauts. Union Jacks. A new jubilee. Just jaw-dropping, tbh. All this jitteriness. All this jingoism. Joblessness. QAnon jargon. Jiminy Crickets. Just waiting for the next shoe to fall, the next cop to fall, the next barricade to fall. Jumping for joy. It's all just so jubilant. Four white words jackhammered to their heads. A white jamboree.

Any kind of king is still a king. Any kind of cadaver is still a cadaver. Death knows this, kinda. Undertakers undertake in it, kinda. Priests, kingmakers, queens kept by their kings. Kinships. The king's ships. Kingfishers. The kiss of death. Fly the flags with the king's name. Break barricades and windows shouting the king's name. *All Hail, Sieg Heil, Oyez Oyez,* our king. Mandarin headed mandarin. Kiss the ring of the kaiser, kiss the ring of Caesar, kiss the ring of the czar. Kamikazes. Kalashnikovs. Any kind of king is still a caliph. Any kind of king is still a khan. Death has known this for centuries. Sentries know this, kinda. Security guards secure it, kinda. Flags fly with the monarch's coat of arms. Chanting the king's name. Shrieking the king's name, again and again. Trump Towers. Trump University. Trump National Golf Club. Donald J. Trump State Park. Repeat after me. Any kind of king is still a kingdom. Dukes. Oligarchs. Rise. Repeat. Overlords. Autocrats. Dons. Any kind of king is still a king.

Let the great neighbors in, the all lives matter people. Let Dominic Pezzola, Proud Boy and former U.S. Marine from Rochester, NY, bash in a Capitol window with a stolen police shield. Looks like bros in a barroom, like bruhs in a brouhaha. We've seen the flags already, the red MAGA hats and all the camouflage. We're seeing the Capitol breached for the first time since the War of 1812. Rubber bullets. Blood on the floor at the front of the police line. Someone screams ***Kill Nancy Pelosi!*** Someone yells ***Hang Mike Pence!*** Every sentence is an exclamation. Look, Trump atop a tank flag. Look, white lives flooding the white marble stairs. All this white matter. It matters again. It's all that has ever mattered in America, tbh. Lust for land. Lust for capital. Lust for the U.S. Capitol. Flood gates unfurling, bike racks flying aside, so much yelling and hollering. Look, they really are such great neighbors. Pezzola owns a flooring company at the edge of Lake Ontario, but he's never seen white waves like these. So prepare to light the streetlamps as dusk lurks on the timeline. They've arrived and plan to stay a while, like it or not.

MAKE AMERICA GASP AGAIN MAR-A-LAGO AMERICAN GRANDSTANDING AGAIN MACABRE AMERICA GYRATE AGAIN MAXIMIZE AMERICAN GODS AGAIN MALCONTENT AMERICAN GRINGOS AGAIN MAQUILADORA AMERICAN-MADE GARMENTS AGAIN MERCILESS AMERICA GIMMEGIMME AGAIN MASTURBATE AMERICAN GLORYHOLES AGAIN MOAN AMERICA GROAN AGAIN MELTDOWN AMERICAN GRUESOMENESS AGAIN MUCKRAKING AMERICA GERRYMANDER AGAIN MEMORIALIZE AMERICAN GUYS AGAIN MUTATE AMERICAN GENTS AGAIN MOGULS AMERICAN GREED AGAIN MADHATTERS AMERICAN GUILLOTINES AGAIN MOCK AMERICA GUFFAW AGAIN MALICIOUS AMERICAN GRUBINESS AGAIN MAGNIFY AMERICAN GRAVITAS AGAIN MEGAPHONING AMERICAN GRAYBEARDS AGAIN MUSTER AMERICAN GRUDGES AGAIN MANSPLAIN AMERICAN GROUNDSWELLS AGAIN MENACING AMERICAN GROUPTHINK AGAIN MUTILATE AMERICA GENUFLECT AGAIN MULTIBARRELED AMERICAN GRIEVANCES AGAIN MEANWHILE AMERICAN GRENADES AGAIN MOSTLY AMERICAN GRAVEYARDS AGAIN MAKE AMERICA GUNS AGAIN M16 AR-15 GLOCK 19X AGAIN MULTIPLY AMERICAN GRAVESTONES AGAIN MANUFACTURE AMERICAN GHOSTS AGAIN

Notice how the great white neighbors join the great white American men. *American Army Entering the City of Mexico* (frieze painted in grisaille), *Andrew Jackson* (statue, bronze). No one could be greater. Not the great white neighbor carrying a Confederate flag. Not the white man carrying a Louisville slugger. *Baptism of Pocahontas* (oil on canvas), *Christopher Columbus* (relief sculpture, sandstone). Inside, the narrow white hallways are becoming even narrower now. All the hats are MAGA hats. So nice, so neighborly. Such great Americans, all finally unmasked. ***Mike Pence didn't have the courage . . .*** , Trump tweets, ***. . . to protect our Country and our Constitution.*** National negligence, natural law. *Colonization of New England* (frieze painted in grisaille, again), *Conflict of Daniel Boone and the Indians, 1773* (relief sculpture, sandstone, again). Nuclear launch codes. Nullifications. Numbness. White noise. *Ulysses S. Grant* (statue, marble). *Gerald R. Ford, Jr.* (statue, bronze). Greatness? *Naval Gun Crew in the Spanish-American War* (frieze painted in grisaille, again).

Oath Keepers overwhelm the cops at the U.S. Capitol. QAnons overwhelm the cops at the U.S. Capitol. Proud Boys overwhelm the cops at the U.S. Capitol. Our ex-U.S. Marines overwhelm the cops at the U.S. Capitol. A bunch of far-right Republicans overwhelm the cops at the U.S. Capitol. And the Neo-Cons overwhelm the cops at the U.S. Capitol. And the Neo-Fascists overwhelm the cops at the U.S. Capitol. And the Neo-Nazis overwhelm the cops at the U.S. Capitol. Everybody is trying to overthrow the U.S. Capitol. Everyday white Americans, most in MAGA hats. The National Guard is AWOL. It's only crowds, throngs, and mobs. It's eye-opening, tbh. The livestreams on Verizon, Fox News, and Patriot Mobile show the cops being overwhelmed at the U.S. Capitol. You can hear and see the bombs and flash bangs, the tear gas and rubber bullets bursting in this January air. No ospreys or snowy owls, but the obituaries, they are just beginning. Locate the origins of America in its oligarchies, its ostracisms. Locate the origins of America in its xenophobia. The origins of America, o'er the land of the free and the home of the brave, that we've occupied since the onset. You don't see it all too often quite honestly. Cops overwhelmed at the U.S. Capitol.

"Helmet Boy" Zachary Alam, Trump supporter from Pennsylvania, punches a glass panel window with a helmet he grips in his right hand, a red MAGA cap grasped in his left. It's pantomime and it's pithy. A particular continuum of a particularly American past of pilfering and pillage. Zachary Alam pledging his allegiance to the republic for which he pounds on a Capitol glass window and shatters it. Welcome home, pugilists. Just don't trust the priests or the police. Don't trust the process or the presidents. Just feel the palpitations, the pointlessness. The pulse of certain precincts and prisons that continue to persevere across America. A Trumper inside the United States Capitol shouting ***Tell fucking Pelosi we're coming for her!*** Zachary Alam howling ***Fuck the blue! Fuck the blue!*** Pretending to be patriots. *E pluribus unum*. Puh-lease. What we're watching is pretty much American history and it's here to reap its rewards. Pulverizing the public sphere. And growing in popularity. Helmet Boy. Proud Boys. Neo-fascists and neo-Nazis. Oh you pretty things. Here to punctuate your emperor. Here to prop up your king.

Conquerors Conquistadors **QAnon** Frequent Prequels

QAnonNarratives Quarrels Quagmires Quarantines **QBreadcrumbs**

QDrops Frequent Queries Inquiries Bouquets **QAnonSlogans**

QAnonLevelClearance Mystique Marquees Quarrelsome Quirks

QAnonpeddledchildsextraffickingconspiracies Qualify Quantify

QAnonMemePostedbyEricTrump Frequent Soliloquies Quests

NoQuestionsPlease **QAnonFollowers** **QAnonSupportingAccounts** Obliquely

Opaque **QSpeak** **QAwareness** AnEnragedQueue AntiqueGlassandWindows

Piqued Torqued **QueenBeeAsh** SquadronoftheUnitedStatesAirForce Iraq

Qatar **QClearancePatriot** Unequaled Quickening Quivering

QAnonfollowers EarthquakeLike **QAnonymous** Quashed Quelched

Quelled **#Q** EquippedwithFlexcuffs **FAQs** **Q&As** Inadequacies

Delinquencies Bouquets **Q+** **GiantQ** **17Anon** Ventriloquists

Disquieters Quieter QuieterStill **QAmericans** Mosquitoes Requisite

QAnons Relinquishing Relinquished FuneralBouquets

If there's still an America after today, ravens will devour it. Ravens feed on garbage on the outskirts of the suburbs, follow wolves in the wilderness, peck at the remains of a roadside carcass of a deer. Great white neighbors invade the Capitol rotunda. Q-Shaman poses his superior posture upon the dais. Remember this. The ravens are watching. They feed on live and dead birds, bird eggs, doves and pigeons, kittiwakes and terns and murrelets, flickers and woodpeckers. Outside the Capitol building, one white mister, a red Trump 2020 scarf draped around his neck, blows a kudu horn. Another great white neighbor in an aqua QAnon hoodie shouts, ***We the People! We are the storm!*** Soon there will be thunder and ice. Predictions of freezing rain. Everywhere there are Gadsden rattlesnakes. Everywhere there are rats. Ravens know this. They eat locusts, ants, scorpions, snails, slugs. Renegades? Rebels? Roadkill. A Blue Lives Matter flag rips through this early January wind. A raven whistling, or just after.

Spew fake news. Nonsense scenarios and fire extinguishers. Surges and scrums. Trumpers shouting, ***Take your pig sorry asses and go back up in there!*** Star-spangled banners. Star-studded newscasters with such impeccable anchor hair. Rush Limbaugh. Sean Hannity. Tucker Carlson. Séance of strongmen, sadomasochists, skeptics. Male sterility and so many blistering white screeds. Patriot Party of Mississippi sign. Presidential Seal. Replacement theories. A red plastic garbage can is carried aloft through this not-so-subtle January air. White men in red MAGA sweatshirts. Vehement multitudes. Savage masses. Scarecrows of the past. Pontius Pilates. Soldiers and self-proclaimed centaurs. Pitiless. Possessed. *Trump 2020* flag slung across a long metal pole is used as a battering ram. Same with a plastic shield. Same with a hockey stick, the shaft of a crutch. Same with the pole of the American flag. Everyone is swinging something. Everyone is screaming. ***Stop the Steal! Stop the Steal!*** Safeguarding their salvation, their savior. Trying so hard to save their king. So many great seeds are being sown here today. Sown in the wind and gone with the wind yet again. See all the MAGA hats. Scarlet red, blood-like. Sewn in the US of A.

Take away the riot helmets and riot gear. Take away the MAGA hoodies and MAGA hats. Take away the torchlights, the troopers, the teeth. Especially all the white teeth. Take away the Gadsden timber rattlesnake flag that Rosanne Boyland, 34, wears across her back. Take away the shopping mall gift kiosk in Kennesaw, Georgia, where she wrapped Christmas gifts. Take away her felony drug-related offenses, her cervical cancer. Take away everybody's fucking cancer while we're at it. Sometimes people need a savior. An intercessor. A Golden Knight. A King. OK his hair is mandarin but still. It's taxing. It's abhorrent. A history of opiates and heroin abuse. AA. Twelve steps. Tainted and tarnished past. Ten times a day posting QAnon and pro-Trump messages. Take away the tomahawk chops. Take away this thunder, this storm. Take away the toxic tinctures. Reddit, Twitter, Truth Social, Parler. Take away the mobs of great white neighbors chanting ***I can't breathe! I can't breathe!*** Take away their MAGA hats, their teeth, their boots, take away their teeth and boots, their bone-crushing boots, their teeth and lung-crushing boots, their bones and their boots, their boots, their boots, their boots, their boots, their boots, their boots . . .

Underneath this inferno is a history of hate. Creatures from the underworld. Aeacus, Acheron. Uninhibited and unmasked. White silhouettes. A particularly American underbelly of ulcers. Unfounded assertions. Amurica unhinged. Amurica undone. An underside of slurs and assaults. Underdogs? German Shepherds, Siberian Huskies, Cerberus. The rotunda in utter mayhem. Outrageous rage. Maybe there will be truncheons. Seagulls circling under the dusky skies. Maybe public torture. Too much? Unlikely. Here it's Charon, Erebus. Covered under army fatigues, flannel shirts, MAGA hats, baseball bats, great white neighbors chanting, ***Hang Mike Pence! Hang Mike Pence!*** Uncertain States of America. Unsteady and Unstable. States Unashamed. Unfortunately it's more like Hades here, more like Hypnos, like the Lethe. Unpaid bills. Underwater mortgages. Underestimated wrath. So ugly but not so uncommon. We know they've brought a noose, brought a hanging platform. Unalterable is their belief in their king.

Sedition has always been in the vocabulary. Like vampires. Like turkey vultures who swoop down upon an already dead deer. Sedition, from the late Middle English, *violent strife*. So much vitriol. Covid vaccinations. So much has been unmasked. From the Latin, *sed (apart)* & *ition (-ire, going)*. Vagabonds and visionaries. Vandals and ventriloquists. So many vowels and violations. ***I was invited here by the President!*** Not shrinking violets but growing violence. Storms, viceroys, to the victors go the spoils. Spoiled brats. Vacant and vacated lives. In the vicinity where their beliefs might go unvanquished. Vanguards of past power. Advocates of today's havoc. Volatile. Vulgar. But the skies are beginning to darken now as the daylight begins to vanish. Clouds of tear gas begin to wash over waves upon waves of great white men who still vie to preserve their overlord, their kingdom, their king. They were so very close, almost on the verge of it. Except for the widespread vendettas. Unacknowledged vulnerabilities. Venture capital. It's all so very American. All the vermin. Vexations. And all that American venom. It's so vast. Old volcanoes spewing volcanic ash.

Winter winds whirl outside. Great white neighbors beginning to wither away. From the thirteen colonies to the Wayfair conspiracy. QAnon. Infowars.com. George Washington, Warren Harding, Woodrow Wilson, George H. W. Bush, George W. Bush. 45. As it's been writ upon the white pages of history. Great neighbors. Just one of the guys. *It's a Wonderful Life.* Wonder Bread. Grant Wood's 3-pronged pitchfork. Someone with a MAGA hat. Witch Trials. Vietnam War. Shock and Awe. American wages. Westerns. *Storm Warning. Dark Victory.*

Foxes entered the hen house. X-Men arrived in camouflage, extremely red MAGA caps. Quixotic. Explosive until the oxygen runs out. America's expiring now. Great neighbors aghast. Just look at the history texts. The galaxy in which they were great patriots making America great again is being evacuated now. Everybody's beginning to exit now. The crux of this violent coaxing has been nixed. Lights alight inside the windows against this dimming daylight. It's an anti-climax. Wanted to play in the sandbox and played in the sandbox. Imagined they would expunge the election, restore their noble king, exonerate and exalt his name. American exceptionalism. Yet another exclusion. Another wasted flex. *And thus were the evening and the morning of the sixth day.*

Yes, tear gas and flash bangs disperse the mob on the inauguration terrace. Yes, the yowling continues. And yes, dusk comes as it always does. Yellow-vested cops who are beginning to matter again. ***Great patriots,*** Trump calls the great white neighbors in a tweet. ***Remember this day forever.*** Yesterday is further away than tomorrow. The naysayers still naysaying but quieter now, the outyelled still out yelling but quieter too. Soothsayers soothsaying. Betrayers still betraying. Yes, eyelashes still lash at the dimming of the day. Dashing out the fires on the stairs of the United States Capitol. What has burned has burned yet there is still so much more to burn. So yoke the oxen to the New Year (it's only six days old). Years from now, history will still look like history. The voice-over might even say that the yardsticks have been moved. You'll stream it on YouTube.

Zeitgeist of the (white) American era. Zoom out from Zachary Taylor to Pizzagate. Zoom in to zero, zilch. A great neighbor in a red MAGA hat holds a bronze statue of a Trump bust aloft in his left hand. Sign of the times. Bedazzlements, embezzlements, a blizzard of huzzahing white neighbors. So great. Or maybe just the unleashing of the zealots. Maybe just the unmuzzling of the buzzards. Again. The buzz of the streetlights as night comes on. It will still get darker and darker still. Cue the harps and the zithers. Cast the bronze sarcophagus. Zenith to zed.

Stateline
Bullets
Reloading Supplies
15 Kilrow St.
Great Bend, PA
(570) 871-7900
www.statelinebullets.com
CALL
MAIN STREET
KILROW ST

SPRING

America makes its own assassins. A2 flash hider: $10 Manufactures them anywhere and everywhere. Arisaka/Modlite 18650 series: $220-$440 Just ask Uncle Sam. Aimpoint PRO: $450 Aimpoint T-2: $800 America made this boy. Aimpoint Comp M5: $871 Aero Precision AR-15 stripped lower: $93 Admit it. Aero Precision M4E1 stripped lower: $125 His all-encompassing whiteness. Aero Precision AR-15 stripped upper: $70 Aero Precision ME41 stripped upper: $115 Aero Precision lower parts kits: $35-$80 Aero Precision upper parts kit: $21 His Bushmaster AR-15. American Trigger gold adjustable trigger: $270 A2 pistol grip: $5 Aero Precision Enhanced Carbine Buffer Kit: $60 His body armor. Aero Precision M4E1 Threaded Assembled Receiver Set: $240 Aero Precision AR-15 Lower Parts Kit, Minus FCG/Trigger Guard/Pistol Grip: $35 Made the Second Amendment. Advanced Combat Helmet (older aramid variant): $150-$250 Avon Protection BA3A Ballistic Helmet: $279.99 White nationalists on 4chan, 8chan. ArmorSource AS-600 Helmet: $949.99 In basements and bedrooms. Avon Protection L110 Combat II Helmet: $1,550 AWS 50735 IFAK pouch: $30 Another Blue Lives Matter flag. On Amber Hill Road. Arc'teryx LEAF Gen II Assault Shirt: $270 Aglite K19: $220 AWS Operator Hybrid: $255 Another birthday, another anniversary, another massacre. AWS Operator Choice: $290 Arc'teryx LEAF Assault Pant gen II: $252 It's automatic. It's a semi-automatic. AWS 50725 LAB belt: $74 AXL Eclipse belt: $115 Arc'teryx LEAF H150 Riggers Belt: $129 Say Uncle. AWS 50771 SMU belt: $148 It's America. Asolo Fugitive GTX: $285 Asolo Arctic GV: $300

Bullets don't believe in anything. Bushmaster XM-15 E2S: ($832.02-$1,200.99) BCM GunFighter Compensator mod 0 or 1: $100 Bravo Company MCMR: $180-$200 BCM QRF: $185-$200 Blue Force Gear Vickers sling: $55 Buffalo Buffalo Buffalo Buffalo Buffalo Buffalo Buffalo Buffalo. Burris RT-6 1-6x24: $350 Brownells BRN-15 M4 stripped lower: $70 Brownells BRN-15 M4 stripped upper: $70 BCM M4 stripped upper: $119 BCM Commercial Lower Parts Kit: $50 We bleed the same blood, yet only some of us are bleeding. Brownells Lower Parts Kit w/ Trigger Assemblies: $58 BCM GunFighter Enhanced Lower Parts Kit: $120 BCM BCG Auto: $189 Brownells AR magazine: $15 B5 Type 23 pistol grip: $20 BCM GunFighter options: $18-$25 Brownells M4 buttstock: $22 BCM GunFighter Options: $55-$60 The city, Buffalo. The animal, once almost extinct, the buffalo. B5 Systems BRAVO: $60 BCM Buffer Kit: $60 B5 Systems BRAVO stock: $58 Black Nitrile Gloves: ($4.79) Bunch of Spongebob band aids ($3.61) A verb, to buffalo. Beez Combat Systems IFAK pouch: $30 To intimidate. Blue Force Gear Trauma Kit NOW! options: $45-$100 To bully. Basic 3M safety glasses: $10-$30 Ballistic Z87 + Pit Vipers: $110 To be buffaloed. Beez APTUM: $210 Beez ESAPI plate carriers: $200-$268 To be broken. Beez Combat Systems BALCS Cumber Grid: $300 Beez AR/AK chest rig: $78-$88 Blue Force Gear ten-speed chest rig: $96 Blue Force Gear MOLLEminus chest rig: $130 Beez Shihan chest rig: $166 We lie in our bed on your birthday, and the news from Buffalo screams across the flatscreen. Blackhawk Black Kryptek Closed Tripe Magazine Pouch: $3 Beez Combat Systems GRIDLOK: $31 Tops Friendly Markets in the Fruit Belt. Beez Combat Systems ARES: $37 Blue Force Gear Ten-Speed: $54 Beez Combat Systems GRIDLOK: $30 The death bouquets are just beginning to be brought here, my beloved. Blue Force Gear Triple: $70 Blue Force Gear Flapped Ten-Speed: $80 Black Sun Patches: ($4.00-$9.99) Blue Force Gear CHLK belt: $250 Ballston: $15 Belleville USGI surplus boots: $20-$80 Buffalo Buffalo Buffalo Buffalo Buffalo Buffalo Buffalo Buffalo.

Conklin, New York. Broome County. Centurion C4 Picatinny Rails: $280-$320 Cloud Defensive Rein: $300 Conklin Castle. On Conklin Road. Built in 1900 by farmer-artist Alpheus Corby. CMMG Zerod Ambidextrous charging handle: $80 CMMG stripped lower: $100 CMMG upper parts kit: $23 CMC triggers: $190-$240 Cryptic Coatings BCG's: $117-$450 Carol McKinstry converted the castle into the Valentino Memorial Church of Psychic Fellowship. Carol claimed Valentino came to her each night and dictated an 80,000 page film script. She moved to Hollywood from Conklin. Her film was never made. Crye Airframe Helmet: $1,092.70-$1,132.00 Conklin Castle became a charity house, a community space, a casualty (almost) of the 2006 and 2011 catastrophic floods. Crye Precision Platebag Soft Armor Insert: $153.90 Crye LVS Base Vest: $850 Crye Side Soft Armor Insert: $48.90 Conklin, the same Congressional district as us, US 19. Dick's Distribution Center, Amazon Flex, FedEx. Cheap Foldable Mossy Oak Knife: ($9.99) CAT-7 tourniquets (1 in each front trouser pocket): ($59.08) A Conklin cul-de-sac. Crime scene cameras. Comtac III/Comtac XP: $600-$800 Comtac V: $600-$800 Comtac VI: $750-$1,200 The carnage at Christchurch. For breakfast, corned beef hash. Patrick Crusius. Canisius College (my alma mater, a possible target). Rochester Walmart (a possible target). Syracuse (a possible target). Black America (the target). *Mis Corazónes* (the targets). Crye Precision G3 Combat Shirt: $150-$180 Crye Precision G4 Combat Shirt: $185 Crye Precision JPC 2.0 Multicam Black w/ AVS Detachable Flap: $266.10 A crock pot in Conklin, New York. Crye Precision AirLite SPC: $169 A couch, cushions. A chair where all this hate was consumed. Crye Precision JPC 1.0: $210 Crye Precision JPC 2.0: $242 Crye Precision CAGE Plate Carrier: $392 Used cars in the parking lot. Crye Precision AVS Base rig: $600 Crye AirLite chest rig: $197 Writing in high school that he wanted to commit a murder-suicide. Crye AVS detachable chest rig: $400 Crye Precision AVS Detachable Flap: $101 Discord. 4chan. Crye Precision G3 Combat Pants: $274 Racist screeds. Crye Precision G4 Combat Pants: $279 or $346 (flame resistant) One day he crosses the threshold. Crosses burning. Continues firing. Could only describe the shooter as a (white) shadow. Crye Precision Range belt: $135 From Conklin. Crye Precision MRB 2.0: $151

Family Dollar. Dragon Kim. Dead Air flash hider: $89 Conklin Reliable Market where the killer once worked. Daniel Defense Superior Suppression Device: $66 Daniel Defense Gen II Muzzle Climb Mitigator: $77 Binghamton Rifle Club just up Conklin Road. Daniel Defense WAVE muzzle brake: $144 Daniel Defense Omega: $222-$244 Dropped off 5 boxes of ammunition at a friend's house. Daniel Defense MFR: $300-$333 Daniel Defense DDM4: $407-$440 Daniel Defense RIS II: $476 Rabid Discord posts. Repeated references to white supremacist memes. Daniel Defense Lower Receiver Parts Kit: $113 Daniel Defense Complete Bolt Carrier Group: $217 Once the dam breaks the dam breaks. Daniel Defense Collapsible Buttstock: $78 Daniel Defense Carbine Buffer Kit: $90 Daytime recedes from the hills and night comes down in the valleys. Daniel Defense 11.5" 5.56mm, carbine, 1:7 GOV barrel w/ low profile gas block: $338 The landscape doesn't make us accomplices but maybe sometimes its history does. Drifire FR combat shirt: $120 Defense Mechanisms MEPC: $235 Defense Mechanisms AR Mag Placard: $50 Duluth Trading Go Buck Naked: $23 Domestic terrorists. Darn Tough: $20-$32 Life on a dead-end road.

Erie County. EOtech EXPS2 or XPS3: $580 EOtech EXPS3 or XPS 3: $700 EOtech Vudu 1-6x25: $1,300-$1,400 E. Utica St., Memphis Alley. ELCAN SpecterDR 1-4x32: $1,900 EOtech XPS-3 w/ LaRue Tactical EOtech QD Mount LT110: $866 Enhanced Combat Helmet: $400-$700 Laurel, Riley, Kingsley. ESAPI Level IV or IV + ICW Plates: $200-$500 ESBI Level IV or IV + ICW Plates: $100-$200 Eye Cups: ($3.39) Jefferson Avenue. Esstac Daeodon: $250. Eagle Industries multi-mission chest rig: $150-$170 Esstac KYWI: $23-$33 Eagle Industries series: $30-$34 Early afternoon. Esstac KYWI Triple: $65-$86 ExOfficio Give-N-Go 2.0 Boxer Briefs: $20-$32 ESSTAC Enhanced Shooter's Belt: $110 Live on Eyewitness News. Eagle Industries Operators gun belt: $108-$141 Ellsworth: $21-$26

Frantic screams floating in the sky. Ferro Concepts Slingster: $58 Like the sound of fireworks, the sound of a firing squad. 5.56x45 Winchester 55gr FMJ: ($13.99) Ferro Concepts Ceramic Composite Special Threat: $362.50-$389.50 Firing a modified semi-automatic rifle. Ferro Concepts roll 1 trauma pouch: $85 The first 30 seconds, the final 30 seconds. First Tactical Defender: $100 Ferro Concepts Slickster: $160 Footage from a body cam. Ferro Concepts Turnover: $24 Dear heavenly father. Ferro Concepts KTS: $75 Dear Furies, dear redacted F.B.I. files. First Tactical Defender: $100-$160 Forget the funereal bouquets. FjällRäven Vidda Pro: $165 Five minutes from Forest Lawn Cemetery. Five minutes from the final resting place of Shirley Chisholm and Rick James. Ferro Concepts Bison belt: $215 Forgotten elders, forgotten graves.

Griffin Armament FlashComp: $110 Golden larches gild the hillsides. Geissele MK8 or MK14: $275-$300 They'll go gold again under autumn's death watch, but today they're green in spring's growing light. Geissele Super charging handle: $105-$115 Geissele Super Duty Lower Parts Kit: $105 Geissele Ultra Duty Lower Parts Kit: $145 Geissele SSA or SSA-E trigger: $240 "My grandmother went to buy seeds for her garden." Geissele SSA X or SSA-E X trigger: $325 Geissele Enhanced Bolt Carrier Group: $370 Geissele Super 42 Spring and Buffer Assembly: $65 Gilded Age, gilded body armor. Galvion Caiman Bump Helmet System: $525 Galvion Caiman Hybrid Helmet System: $875 Gentex TBH-IIIA Mission Configured Helmet System: $640 Red flags. Online groomers. Funeral gowns. Galvion A-Series Helmets: $525.14 Galvion P-Series Helmets: $1078.41-$1,219.08 Galvion Ballistic Helmet System: $1,749.99 White male, 19 goddamn years old. Galvion Viper Modular Suspension System (MSS): $169.00-$197.42 Galvion Viper Front Mount and Viper Interlocking Long Rails: $185.98 A golden age? GoPro Hero7 Black: ($298) Gerber Strap Cutter: ($29.39) Gerber Multitool: ($28.99). GRBS Group Assaulter Belt System V2: $255 GORUCK MACV-1 series boots: $120-$160 Golden smoke from an illegally modified AR-15.

America is a heavy casket, a black hearse. Haley Strategic D3 sling: $100 Holosun 403 series: $206-$258 Holosun 503 series: $294-$341 Holosun 510 series: $365-$400 He said he had an AR-15. Holosun HE512: $420-$620 Handwritten names and neo-Nazi symbols on his rifle. Hiperfire HiperTouch triggers: $190-$260 Hogue INC options: $20-$30 HK V2 pistol grip: $40 He wore a HAZMAT suit to high school. Highcom ULACH Series Helmets: $656 Highcom Striker Arditi (RCH) Helmet: $2,399.00-$2,703.40 Beheaded a feral cat. Highcom Striker ACH-ARC Rail System: $105.00 Highcom Striker Ballistic Visor: $449 Highcom SA 3100 Plate Backer: $145 His rampage. His high-capacity ammunition. Hoplite 19300: $149 Hate in his heart. Hesco P210: $159-$252 Hesco 3402: $443.00 Highcom 3s11: $417-$507 Highcom 3s11m: $558.95-$858.95 His helmet. His handguns. Hoplite 23620: $700-$800 Hesco 3800C: $392.99-$535.99 Hesco L210: $$169.60 Hesco M210: $309-$464 Hesco U210: $875-$943 Haunting flea markets and military surplus stores. Highcom 3s9: $468-$569 Highcom 3s9m: $447.50 Hoplite 19513: $390 Hesco 3611C: $435-$490 Hesco 3810 III + Plate: $502-$912 He was right here, *my dear.* On this very asphalt. Hoplite 26225-26226: $162.50-$187.50 Highcom Guardian 4s17: $179 Highcom Guardian 4s17m: $215-$296 Highcom 4sas7: $195-$237.50 Homeland Security. Hoplite 26605: $265-$339 Hesco 4601: $486-$711 Highcom 4s16: $319-$389 Highcom 4sss2: $848.95-$1,208.95 Hoplite 26300: $1,500-$1,687.50 Hoplite 29590: $2,000 Hesco 4800: $1,153-$1,504 Hoplite 19301: $75 He was 18 years old. Hesco BI P110: $75-$100 He was 17 years old. Hesco BI 3100: $189 He was 19 years old. Hoplite 23526: $337.50 He was 20 years old. Hesco BI 3100: $233-$262 He was 23 years old. Highcom 4s17: $142.50 He was 24 years old. Hoplite 26227-26228: $150 He was 26 years old. Hesco BI 4101: $300-$400 He was 28 years old. H&H H bandages: ($8.98) H&H Compression Gauze: ($15.55) H&H Sterile Burn Dressing: ($7.95) He was 29 years old. HSGI ReVive medical pouch: $76 He was 46 years old. Howard Leight Impact Sport models: $50-$120 Haley Strategic D3CRX: $200 He was 64 years old. HSGI TACO or Duty series: $39 He was 72 years old. HSGI Taco series: $107-$133 HSGI TACO Covered: $49

. . . in Allen, Texas in Annapolis, Maryland in Appomattox, Virginia in Arvada and Colorado Springs, Colorado in Ascension and Livingston Parish, Louisiana in Atlanta and Cherokee County, Georgia in Austin and Bexar County, Texas in Aurora, Colorado in Aurora, Illinois in Bakersfield, California in Baton Rouge, Louisiana in Binghamton, New York in Blacksburg, Virginia in Boulder, Colorado in Brookfield, Wisconsin in Broward County, Florida in Buffalo, New York in Burlington, Washington in Carnation, Washington in Carson City, Nevada in Carthage, North Carolina in Casas Adobes, Arizona in Centerville and Jourdanton, Texas in Charleston, South Carolina in Charlotte, North Carolina in Chattanooga, Tennessee in Chesapeake, Virginia in Chicago and Evanston, Illinois in Citronelle, Alabama in Cleveland, Texas in Columbus, Ohio in Copley Township, Ohio in Covina, California in Crandon, Wisconsin in Dallas, Texas in Dayton, Ohio in DeKalb, Illinois in Denver and Lakewood, Colorado in East Lansdowne, Pennsylvania in El Paso, Texas in Enoch, Utah in Fort Hood, Texas in Fresno, California in Geneva and Samson, Alabama in Gilbert, Arizona in Goleta, California in Goshen, California in Grand Rapids, Michigan in Half Moon Bay, California in Harris County, Texas in Henderson, Kentucky in Henryetta, Oklahoma in Hialeah, Florida in Highland Park, Illinois in Indianapolis, Indiana in Irving, Texas in Isla Vista, California in Jersey City, New Jersey in Joliet, Illinois in Kalamazoo, Michigan in Kansas City, Kansas in Kirkwood, Missouri in Lewiston, Maine in Lincoln County, Mississippi in Louisville, Kentucky in Manchester, Connecticut in Marysville, Washington in Meteor, Wisconsin in Milwaukee, Wisconsin in Minneapolis, Minnesota in Mohawk and Herkimer, New York in Monterey Park, California in Montgomery County, Missouri in Montgomery County, Pennsylvania **Improved H-nape Retention Chinstrap for ACH or ECH: $20-$30** in Muskogee, Oklahoma in Nashville, Tennessee in Newtown, Connecticut in New York City, New York in Nickel Mines, Pennsylvania in Oak Creek, Wisconsin in Oakland, California in Omaha, Nebraska in Orinda, California in Orlando, Florida in Paradise, Nevada in Parkland, Florida in Parkland, Washington in Pearcy, Arkansas in Philadelphia, Pennsylvania **iPhone 11: ($304.47)** in Pittsburgh, Pennsylvania in Plano, Texas in Raleigh, North Carolina in Red Lake, Minnesota in Roseburg, Oregon in Sacramento, California in Saipan, Northern Mariana Islands in San Bernardino, California in San Jose, California in San Juan, Puerto Rico in Seal Beach, California in Sebring, Florida in Skagit County, Washington in Salt Lake City, Utah in Santa Fe, Texas in Scottsdale, Arizona in Seattle, Washington in South Valley, New Mexico in Spring, Texas in Springfield, Missouri in Sutherland Springs, Texas in Thousand Oaks, California in Tinley Park, Illinois in Toa Baja, Puerto Rico in Tulsa, Oklahoma **ITW FastMag: $30** in Tyrone, Missouri in Uvalde, Texas in Virginia Beach, Virginia in Waco, Texas in Wakefield, Massachusetts in Washington, DC in Wilkinsburg, Pennsylvania in Williamsburg, West Virginia in Yountville, California . . .

Just up Jefferson Avenue. Just across the street from Madina Islamic Center of Buffalo. American Trigger gold adjustable trigger: $270 Just south of a Family Dollar and just north of a Family Dollar. Just been hired at the store. Crye Precision JPC 2.0 Multicam Black w/ AVS Detachable Flap: $266.10 Just south of Utica. Just north of Northampton and Southampton. Just west of Jackson's Soul Food. Crye Precision JPC 1.0: $210 Just had a blank stare. Crye Precision JPC 2.0: $242 Just a minute from Leonardo daVinci High School. 5.56x45 Winchester 55gr FMJ: ($13.99) Just started shooting. Fjällräven Vidda Pro: $165 Just north of Urban Christian Ministries and Greater Refuge Temple of Christ. Just east of McDonald's and Burger King on Main Street and the African American Cultural Center on Masten. Lubricating Jelly and Nasopharyngeal Airway Tube: ($19.99) Just dropping to the floor. Trijicon Credo 1-6x24: $1,000 Just kept shooting. Just wouldn't stop shooting. Trijicon Credi 1-Xx28: $1,100-$1,300 USGI surplus jungle boots: $20-$80 Just a mile from the Dollar Store and the end of Michigan near the Freedom Wall. Winchester 55gr FMJ: ($14.99) Just up from where War Memorial Stadium used to be.

Killers come from everywhere. Knights Armament QDC 3-prong flash suppressor: $124 Killers with AK-15s, white killers with white convictions, KKK-killers. Trained on the internet in their basements or bedrooms by other wannabe killers. Conversations on 4chan. Streaming other killings on X and Twitch. Knights Armament URX: $270-$300 Replacement theory conspiracies. Killers come from Conklin, New York. Knights Armament Corporation RAS: $320-$520 Killjoys. Killers with AK-15s, Bushmaster rifles, playing video games in bedrooms and basements, working at the local market, expanding their hate. Kleptomaniacs or kinsmen or not. Nobody cares until everyone seems to care for a little bit. Clickbait. Knights Armament SR-15 charging handle: $150 Killers come from here and there and over there. Blonde or brunette haired. Killers short and not. Nobody knows, OK maybe a few people suspect. Psych evals. HAZMAT suits. Khul options: $100 The signs are there like STOP signs where most folks stop. Killers? Who can hold all that hate? Who can hold that AK-15, that Bushmaster rifle, that Kalashnikov or crappy .38 special and fire into another person's cranium, another person's face, their skull, their heart. Kavu Moonwalk: $25 Killers can. They come from everywhere.

LANTAC Dragon muzzle brake: $130 Lest you believe that life is lived in peace. LaRue Tactical Lok: $86-$162 LaRue Tactical Slick: $111-$162 LaRue Quad Rail: $212-$282 Livid liars on DLive. Leupold VX Freedom 1.5-4x20: $300 Leupold VX-3HD 1.5-5x20: $700 Leupold MK6 1-6x20: $2,200 Luck of the Irish. Lucky Charms. LWRCI Ambi charging handle: $105-$115 LMT Ambidextrous 5.56 charging handle: $119 Lest you live in a world where whiteness isn't losing its luster. LWRCI Lower Receiver Builder's Kit: $40-$50 LWRCI upper parts kit (comes with mil-spec charging handle): $40 Lucky for you, I guess. LaRue MBT triggers: $100-$120 Unlucky for the rest of US. LMT Full-Auto 5.56 BCG: $229 LMT Full-Auto Enhanced 5.56 BCG: $459 Lancer L5AWM magazine: $16-$22 Lest you believe the Americans weren't kidding when they said "Give me liberty or give me death" while raising a militia. Lubricating Jelly and Nasopharyngeal Airway Tube: ($19.99) LBT small blow-out kit pouch: $85 Consider yourself lucky. Liberator II: $750-$850 LBT 6094: $512 Thank your lucky stars. Lowa Innox Pro series: $175-$235 Lowa Zephyr series: $200-$250 Lowa Ottawa GTX: You lucky devil. $250 Lowa Tibet Superwarm GTX: $460 Dumb luck.

Mass shooters imagine mass shootings. Midwest Industries ULW: $270-$300 Moment by moment. Midwest Industries CRT: $170-$230 Mass violence. Magpul options (there's a lot): $40-$75 A matter of minutes. Magpul gen 2 or 3 magazines: $10-$20 Magpul options: $20-$25 Magpul options: $45-$255 Social media. M855/SS109: ($17.99) M855A1: ($220) M995: ($39) The worst in modern U.S. history. Magpul B.A.D. lever: $30 Magpul MOE K2 pistol grip: $21 Midwest Industries ULW 10.5" handguard: $270 A white male in a hoodie with an AK-47 or an AR-15. Semi-automatics modified with illegal magazines. Mossberg 500: ($392.99-$499.99) Midwest Armor Stinger III-A Soft Armor Panels: $369-$389 March 15. Magpul series: $100-$140 May 15. Mechanic M-PACT: $20-$30 Mechanix FastFit: $10-$30 Magpul series: $30-$65 Meriwool 160 Boxer Briefs: $27 Malcontents. Massif Breeze: $42 Former Marines, ex-military, retired marksmen. Most U.S. or European military pants: $20-$60 Massif Advanced Quarter Zip Combat Shirt: $229 Murderous white men. Massif Hellman: $363 Zombies. Meri Wool Socks: $16 Just ask their mothers. Most European military boots: $15-$60 Merrel MOAB series boots: $120-$170 Land of make believe Merrel Thermo series: $126-$220 and MAGA.

Nightforce ATACR 1-8x24: $2,800 90s era Colt full auto M4 BCG: $200 Nomex Flight Gloves: $15-$20 Noveske NSR: $250-$290 Nightforce NX8 1-8x24: $1,750

A 186-pg manifesto. Ops-Core FAST Bump Helmet: $285 14208. Ops-Core FAST Carbon Helmet: $833.70 Rounds and rounds of ammo stored in high capacity magazines. Ops-Core FAST SF Carbon Composite Helmet: $900 Open sign. Ops-Core FAST LE Helmet: $975 Ops-Core Sentry XP Helmet: $1,765 Opened fire. Ops-Core FAST XP Helmet: $999.98 On closed circuit television. Ops-Core FAST SF Helmet: $1,800 Ops-Core TBH-R1 Helmet System: $2,035 Ops-Core FAST XR Helmet System: $2,100 On Twitch. Ops-Core FAST RF1 Helmet System: $3,249 Ops-Core Head-Loc 4-point H-Nape Chinstrap: $127 Ops-Core LuxPux: $99 On the officer's body cam. Ops-Core ACH OCC-Dial EPP Kit: $60-180 Ops-Core Vented Lux Liner Kit: $360-$389 Ops-Core ARC Rails: $112 On the radio. Ops-Core Skeleton ARC Rails: $100-$122 Shots fired. Ops-Core Multi-Hit Handgun Face Shield: $593.70 OTV/IOTV soft armor or police vest: $100-$300 On the floor near the cooler. Otto NoizeBarrier Range SA: $400 On the floor in aisle four. Otto NoizeBarrier TAC: $665 Ops-Core AMP: $1,080 Oakley M-Frame Alpha w/ clear inserts: ($157.00) On a Monday. Oakley Tombstone: $150 On a Thursday. Oakley M-frame series: $60-$200 Oakley Tan Factory Pilot 2.0 Gloves: ($69.00) Oakley SI series: $25-$30 On a Sunday. Oakley Factory Pilot (Assault): $40-$60 OTV/IOTV/IMTV/SPCS w/ soft armor: $100-$700 Does anyone have eyes on the shooter?

Paid for the body armor with PayPal. Proctor sling: $45 Palmetto State Armory M4A1 stripped lower: $60 Palmetto State Armory lower parts kits: $30-$80 Packages left at the front door of his parents' home on Amber Lane, a dead end street in Conklin. Palmetto State Armory Carbine Buffer Kit: $45 Permits to carry concealed weapons. Public records. Planned meticulously. 186-page manifesto. ProMAX IIIA Ultra-Thin: $499 Such a great place to live. Put up a basketball hoop on the asphalt driveway. Thoughts & prayers again. ProMAX IIIA Ultimate Ultra-Thin: $749 Police. Paramedics. Peltor Sport models: $50-$180 Tops Friendly Markets. PIG FDT series: $50-$80 Pronounced dead is dead. Resting in peace? Patagonia Sender Boxer Briefs: $30 Passed on? Passed away? Please. Slaughtered. People's Socks: $20 There is no place quite like America.

A quiet subdivision. A quiet dead end lane. This place is always so quiet. A large quantity of ammunition. It's so quiet here. Such a quiet neighborhood. Such a quiet boy. A quiet country life. A really nice area and quality of life. Quintessential small town America. Quick Clot Combat Gauze: ($39.88) Quiet home town. Quiet road. Quiet street. He was very quiet. He was just a quiet, smart kid that I wouldn't think he'd be able to do anything like what he did. Quiet student. He was always so quiet. Qore Performance IcePlate EXO: $650 A quiet studious boy. A quiet young man. Very polite and quiet. He was very quiet and left on his own terms. Quietly. The quiet type. So very quiet. It's just so quiet afterwards. Just so quiet here. Really quiet.

Recent American history is so very American. Rugged R3 flash mitigation system: $100 Radian Raptor charging handles: $90-$120 Replace 1275 Jefferson Avenue, Buffalo, with 110 Calhoun Street, Charleston. Rainier Arms upper parts kit: $24 Radian Raptor ambi charging handle: $90 RMA 0226 Gen-2: $99.99 RMA Protego Concealable Soft Body Armor Vest: $499 Replace the Second Amendment which imagined muskets not AR-15s. RMA Contego Concealable Soft Body Armor Vest: $599 RMA 1061-1064: $275-$345 Racist rampage. RMA 1078: $275 Tops Friendly Markets. RMA 1088: $339 RMA 1091-1094: $274.99-$374.99 RMA 1155: $145 RMA 1155MC: $170 Wrote the names of racist murderers on his rifles. RMA 1192: $700 Wrote their names in white paint. RMA 1155SP: $106 Raptor Tactical ODIN belt MK III: $117 Ronin SENSHI belt: $188-$193 Received another 911 call.

Silencerco ASR flash hider: $78 Surefire SF3P flash hider: $149 Surefire WARCOMP CTN: $149 **The Susquehanna River runs across the southern edge of Broome County, New York.** Surefire M300C Scout Light: $300 Surefire M600DF Scout Light: $300 Surplus M16/M4 sling: $10 Standard mil-spec charging handle: $20 Spike's Tactical stripped lowers: $119 Sons of Liberty Gun Works stripped lower: $140 Spike's Tactical M4 stripped upper: $115 **Flows along the Pennsylvania state line.** Surplus military magazines from Colt, Okay Industries, D&H, etc.: $10-$20 Surefeed (suresheed) AR magazines: $11-$13 Salt Lake City M855 62 gr: ($11.99) Surefire WARCOMP Flash Hider: $149 **Gun shops and rifle ranges on either side of the border.** Surefire M600DF w/ Arisaka M-LOK Offset Scout Mount and Unity Tactical M-LOK Hot Button: $377 Savage Axis XP: ($362.99-$466.99) Striker ACH Series Helmets: $433 Standard ACH Pads: $20 **Susquehanna Valley High School sits beside the Susquehanna River.** SKD Armor IIIA Soft Armor Plate Backer: $99.95 Stealth Armor Systems GTX-K-3A CIRAS BALCS Cut Panels: $330-$470 Slate Solutions H3001: $219-$279 Slate Solutions H4001: $415.00-$813.33 **Across the street, across Conklin Road.** Slate Solutions D1652/Tencate Cratus R-3600 SA: $676.67 Slate Solutions H3101: $298-$369 SKD Armor Cummerbund Inserts: $110-$130 Slate Solutions H3101 Side Plate: $130-$150 **A stone's throw southeast of the Binghamton Rifle Club.** Sony SRS-XB13 Speaker: ($58.00) Small Black Sharpie: ($7.49) Surplus USGI IFAK pouch w/ insert: $10-$20 Sordin Supreme Pro-X LED w/ Leather Headband: ($254.02) Sordin Supreme Pro-X models: $220-$300 Safariland Liberator II HP: $300 Swatcon Active 8: $350-$400 Surplus Revision Sawfly glasses: $20-$40 Surplus ESS Crossbow glasses: $30-$40 Surplus Wiley X series glasses: $40-$60 Smith Elite series: $80-$240 Surplus U.S. Army combat shirts: $20-$40 **Smack dab between Bridgewater Evangelical Church** Surplus USMC MARPAT FROG combat shirt: $40-$120 Surplus police BALCS armor carriers: $20-$60 Surplus police BALCS armor carriers w/ issued soft armor: $50-$250 Shellback Banshee: $250 Spiritus Systems LV-119: $300 Shellback Banshee Elite 3.0: $410-$440 **and Christian Community Church of Conklin.** Shaw Concepts V2 ARC: $490 Stealth Armor Systems LVAC: $170 Surplus Chinese Type 56 chest rig: $20-$30 Spiritus Systems micro fight kit: $100-$130 Surus Operations gen II rig: $100-$150 Shaw Concepts ARC chest rig w/ placard: $200 Surus Operations RECCE 1: $242 Surplus USGI magazine pouch: $10 Smartwood Merino Sport Boxer Briefs: $35 Surplus USMC Tier 1 PUG w/ soft armor inserts: $25-$50 **Just 170 miles northwest of Sandy Hook.** Surplus Eagle Industries War Belt w/ suspenders: $50 S&S modular belt (complete set): $224 Smartwool: $16-$26 Surplus Oakley SI Assault boots: $60-$120 Salomon Quest 4D: $280 Salomon Quest Winter: $180

.223 Remington: ($26.67) To drive from Conklin to Buffalo is to drive through Endicott and Appalachia, Trijicon Credo 1-6x24: $1,000 to drive by Tioga Hills Elementary School and Hiawatha Landing. Trijicon Credi 1-Xx28: $1,100-$1,300 Past Tioga Downs Casino Resort and two Tops Friendly Markets in Elmira Toolcraft black nitride BCG: $80 and the Tops Friendly Markets in Bath (you can see it from the highway). Toolcraft DLC BCG: $160.223 Remington varmint ammunition (usually 40-60gr): ($25.19) The Tops in Dansville (also visible from the highway), .223 Remington 63-64 gr SP, B, SB, PP: ($22.99) Team Wendy XFIL LTP Helmet: $274.98 the Tops in Warsaw and East Aurora, two Tops in West Seneca, three Tops in Cheektowaga. Team Wendy XFIL Carbon Bump Helmet: $595 Team Wendy XFIL Ballistic Helmet: $1,109-$1,309 Or if you drive the northern route from Conklin to Buffalo, by three Tops Friendly Markets in Syracuse, Team Wendy XFIL Ballistic SL Helmet: $1,499.98-$1,545.98 four Tops in Rochester, Team Wendy CAM FIT H-Back Retention System: $68 Team Wendy CAM FIT Retention System: $112 the Tops in Batavia right off Thruway exit 48, Team Wendy EPIC Air Liner System: $104.82 Team Wendy Cloudline System: $112.74 the Tops just north of where the Thruway toll booths used to be off Union Road in Williamsville, Team Wendy EXFIL Ballistic Rail 3.0 Retrofit Kit: $55.19 TCCC Card: ($2.00) three Tops in Cheektowaga, T.Rex Arms MED1 pouch: $53-$60 Tactical Tailor Rogue IFAK pouch: $85 T.Rex Arms AC1: $190 and six other Tops locations in Buffalo. T.Rex Arms 556 ready rig: $130 Tactical Tailor chest rigs: $60-$210 T3 Spear chest rig: $212 Download Google Maps and the Telegram app. Tactical Tailor Fight Light: $20 Tarrant and Reddit and Twitch. Tactical Tailor Fight Light: $35 Tunnel vision. T.Rex Arms Orion Outer Belt: $80-$110 Target practice. TYR Tactical Gunfighter belt: $125

USGI aluminum 30-round magazines: ($11.99) USMC HyFin Chest Seal Combo Pack (expired by 8 months): ($17.39) UF PRO Striker series: $150-$164 USGI FLC: $20 Buffalo Buffalo Buffalo UACI ALICE full webbing: $40-$70 USMC surplus FROG trousers: $40-$100 UF Pro Striker series: $218-$301 The underworld of America. USMC surplus Cavu by Ellsworth socks: $6-$15 USGI surplus jungle boots: $20-$80 USMC surplus rat boots: $50-$80 USGI N-1B Mukluk boots w/ liner: $20-$60 USAF Belleville 675 surplus boots: $25-$90 United States of Uvalde. USGI black or white mickey mouse boots: $50-$150

Vortex Crossfire: $220 Vintage firearms shop on Nanticoke Avenue. Vortex SPARC AR: $275 Vortex Crossfire: $220 Vortex Strike Eagle 1-6x24: $300-$400 White villagers. Vortex Strike Eagle 1-8x24: $400-$500 Vortex Razor HD Gen II-E 1-6x24: $1,400 Vortex Razor HD Gen III 1-10x24: $2,500 Vows that it will never happen again. VLTOR Weapon Systems IMOD stock: $90 VLTOR A5 Buffer Spring and Buffer Kit: $80-$100 Vapors of truth. Vendettas. VLTOR A5 complete buffer system w/ H2 buffer: $96 VELCRO Brand Hook Disks: $5.23 The leitmotiv is oblivion. Velocity Systems SLAAP Up-Armor Ballistic Rifle Plate: $99 Velocity System IIIA Soft Armor SAPI-Cut Plate Backers: $150 Private chat groups. Velocity Systems Special Threat Ceramic Plate: $324-$364 Vape shops. Velocity Systems PSA4: $304.99 Delavan Avenue. AreaVibes.com. Vertx Recon combat shirt: $110 Velocity Systems LWPC: $200 Velocity Systems LEPC: $210 Aversion, revulsion, hate. Velocity Systems LPAC/LPAAC: $260 Velocity Systems Assault: $276 Velocity Systems Scarab series: $326-$370 White vigilantes. Velocity Systems UW gen IV chest rig: $210 Velocity Systems Mayflower Pusher UW gen VI chest rig: $225-$240 The leitmotiv is death.

White wigs white-writing the right to bear arms. Walmart duct tape: ($3.88) Winchester 55gr FMJ: ($14.99) WTF Plate Carrier 13: $99 White whales. Wikipedia. WTF Plate Carrier 06: ($39) High wind warnings. Buffalo wings. WTF Plate Carrier 24: $199 I wanted to leave this page completely white but who would understand it? WTF Turnkey 01: $84-$134 WTF Turnkey 05: $91-$150 Whitewashed photographs from Trump rallies, from Buffalo, whitewashed photos from the towns in New York and Pennsylvania where the Buffalo killer bought his AR-15 that another white person legally sold him. White senators and white representatives who uphold these white-written laws. WTF Accessory Panel 04: $64 Walker's Foam Ear Plugs: ($3.99) White cirrus clouds, summer whites, vanilla ice cream, white chalk circles, white teeth, white bones, white ash.

Bushmaster XM-15

Savage Arms Axis XP

XL Hanes Boxer Briefs: ($16.48)

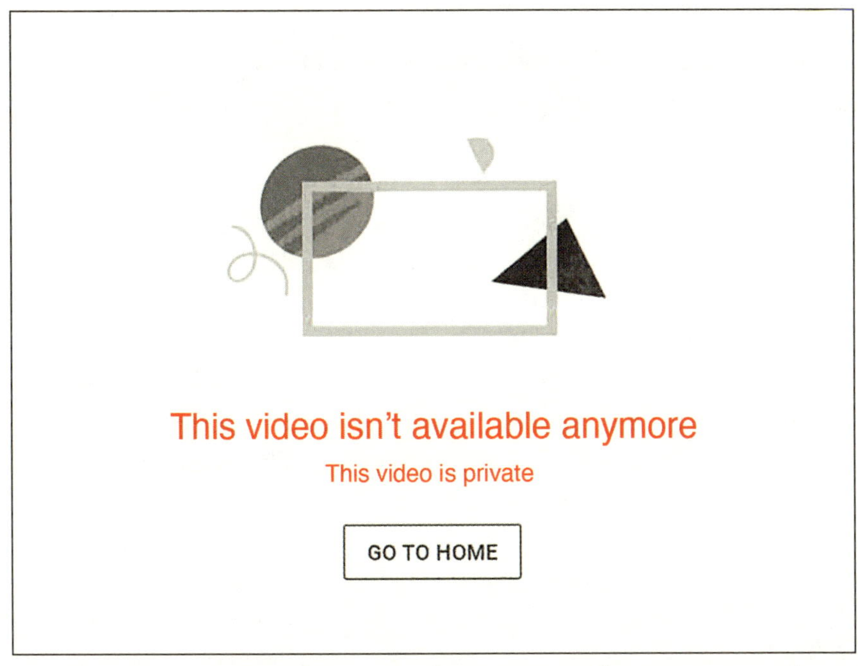

YouTube videos of abandoned churches, empty houses, entropy. AWS Operator Hybrid: $255 B5 Type 23 pistol grip: $20 Crye Precision G4 Combat Shirt: $185 "Check out Emslie, Buffalo," the killer once commented on a video titled *I Drove Through The Worst Parts of Buffalo.* Eye Cups: ($3.39) GRBS Group Assaulter Belt System V2: $255 Haley Strategic D3 sling: $100 It's hidden now, marked "Video unavailable." Lubricating Jelly and Nasopharyngeal Airway Tube: ($19.99) Most European military boots: $15-$60 Whiteness erased by whiteness. Oakley Factory Pilot (Assault): $40-$60 Yet Reclaim Niagara's Facebook page posted the YouTube video a few months later. That post has disappeared now, too. Palmetto State Armory Carbine Buffer Kit: $45 RMA Contego Concealable Soft Body Armor Vest: $599 And WYRK, Country 106.5, reviewed the YouTube video on its page: "When anyone ever says anything bad about Buffalo, we go so defensive. But I could not stop watching this video at all." Surplus U.S. Army combat shirts: $20-$40 TYR Tactical Gunfighter belt: $125 White voyeurs, ex-military men, white trash, white youth. USMC HyFin Chest Seal Combo Pack (expired by 8 months): ($17.39) Velocity Systems SLAAP Up-Armor Ballistic Rifle Plate: $99 WTF Turnkey 05: $91-$150 A *Buffalo News* reporter writes that the YouTube video's white owner, Nick Johnson, who has almost a million subscribers, "did not immediately respond to a request for a comment."

Zombies love to turn everybody into zombies. Brownells AR magazine: $15 Beez Combat Systems IFAK pouch: $30 Ballistic Z87 + Pit Vipers: $110 Beez APTUM: $210 Beez ESAPI plate carriers: $200-$268 Carry semi-automatic weaponz, Beez Combat Systems BLACS Cumber Grid: $300 quiet guyz. Beez AR/AK chest rig: $78-$88 Beez Combat Systems GRIDLOK: $31 Beez Combat Systems ARES: $37 AME Zion Church. Beez Combat Systems GRIDLOK: $30 CMMG Zerod Ambidextrous charging handle: $80 Daniel Defense Gen II Muzzle Climb Mitigator: $77 A flurry of speed zones. Daniel Defense WAVE muzzle brake: $144 The oldest war zone. H&H Compression Gauze: ($15.55) LANTAC Dragon muzzle brake: $130 Lancer L5AWM magazine: $16-$22 "Amazing Grace." Lowa Zephyr series: $200-$250 Magpul gen 2 or 3 magazines: $10-$20 Massif Breeze: $42 Massif Advanced Quarter Zip Combat Shirt: $229 Brazen white nationalist zeal. Another kind of czar. Otto NoizeBarrier Range SA: $400 Otto NoizeBarrier TAC: $665 Quick Clot Combat Gauze: ($39.88) Zombies playing Tarzan again Surplus military magazines from Colt, Okay Industries, D&H, ect: $10-$20 Surefeed (suresneed) AR magazines: $11-$13 Muzzle these new Nazis, muzzle their Panzers again. Surplus USGI magazine pouch: $10 USGI aluminum 30-round magazines: ($11.99) Dead horizons. An endless maze. Vortex Razor HD Gen II-E 1-6x24: $1,400 Vortex Razor HD Gen III 1-10x24: $2,500 Before the first zinnias have had a chance to bloom.

VINTAGE
FIREARMS
LLC
WEST ENDICOTT
&
SUSQUEHANNA
ARMS CO.
BUY - SELL - TRADE
785-3872
Revolvers-Pistols-Military Rifles
TIMBER CREEK
FIREARMS
BUSINESS HOURS

SUMMER

WELCOME TO AMERICA AN UNFINISHED ARMAGEDDON ACTIVE SHOOTER DRILLS FIRE DRILLS FALSE ALARMS AT LEAST AI WRITES OUR THOUGHTS & PRAYERS NOWADAYS AS WE WAIT FOR ANOTHER AXE TO FALL ALLEGHENY ARMS & GUN WORKS ANON AS SHAKESPEARE USED TO SAY TEAR GAS CANISTERS CRIME SCENE TAPE AMBULANCES ALREADY AT HAND A GLASS OF ABSINTHE AN ENVELOPE OF ANTHRAX AMERICAN BITTERSWEET BY THE SIDE OF THE ROAD AN ALBATROSS IS AROUND OUR NECKS AGAIN APPARENTLY IT ISN'T ANTI-AMERICAN TO ASSEMBLE AN ARMY OF ANTI-AMERICANS AMERICAN GLASS RESEARCH ANOTHER MASS SHOOTER ANOTHER AMERICAN MASSACRE & IT ISN'T EVEN AUGUST*

* "AGR [AMERICAN GLASS RESEARCH] INTERNATIONAL IS A WORLD-CLASS, INNOVATIVE SUPPLIER OF QUALITY ASSURANCE AND PROCESS AUTOMATION EQUIPMENT TO THE GLOBAL PACKAGING MARKETS."

BUT BABY SWEET BABY THE HUMMINGBIRDS ARE
BUZZING BY THE BEE BALM AGAIN THE BUTTERFLIES
& THE BEES ARE ABUZZ BY THE BLACK-EYED SUSANS
BUZZING LIKE BULLETS BY THE BITTER DOCK BUTLER
FARM SHOW PODIUM BEAVER COUNTY PENNSYLVANIA
BOMB-MAKING MATERIALS BALLISTIC CALCULATORS
BELIEVE ME THIS IS A BIG BIG BEAUTIFUL CROWD
COMMON BURDOCK BY THE SIDE OF THE ROAD BY
JOVE BYE JOE GOODBYE BON JOVI BUYER BEWARE
IT'S BIGGER THAN A TAYLOR SWIFT CONCERT I'M
THRILLED TO BE BACK HERE THIS IS A BIG BEAUTIFUL
COMMONWEALTH BABY A BIG BEAUTIFUL COUNTRY*

* "IN THE EARLY 1900S, BUTLER WAS A 'STEEL BELT' MANUFACTURING AND INDUSTRIAL AREA . . . LIKE MOST OF THE REGION, BY THE END OF THE 1970S, [BUTLER'S] ECONOMY CHANGED DRAMATICALLY. MANUFACTURING VIRTUALLY ENDED AND WELL-PAYING JOBS BECAME SCARCE . . . THE PULLMAN-STANDARD PLANT CLOSED IN 1982 . . . THE SITE IS NOW OCCUPIED BY A VACANT STRIP MALL."

CIRROSTRATUS CLOUDS IN AN OTHERWISE CLEAR SKY CANADA THISTLE CANADIAN GEESE WE CHAFE AT THE IDEA OF CAUSATION OOPS I MEANT TO SAY CAUCASIAN COMMUNITY COLLEGE OF ALLEGHENY COUNTY COMMON RAGWEED CRABGRASS CREEPING CHARLIE BY THE SIDE OF THE ROAD A CHANCE A CERTAINTY EVERY COUNTRY'S HISTORY CAN ONLY CAUSE A CONFLAGRATION JUST ASK CHINA ASK CHILE JUST ASK THE USA CAUCASIANS AT CLAIRTON SPORTSMEN'S CLUB A CALM SUBURBAN STREET CROCK-POTS COUCHES COFFEE CUPS CASUALTIES CALAMITIES THOMAS MATTHEW CROOKS IF THEY COULD THEY WOULD BE CALLING ALL CARS BUT THAT MY COMRADES IS ANOTHER KIND OF CALLING*

* CROOKS, AKA, THOMAS MATTHEW CROOKS. CERAMICS I: B. COMPUTER KEYBOARDING: A. AP U.S. GOVERNMENT & POLITICS: A. CALCULUS 2: A. CALCULUS 3: B. "THOMAS PLANNED TO GRADUATE FROM CCAC [COMMUNITY COLLEGE OF ALLEGHENY COUNTY] ENGINEERING PRIOR TO TRANSFERRING TO PITT. . . . I ALSO MENTIONED THE CCAC/RMU GATEWAY PROGRAM FOR MECHANICAL ENGINEERING AS THIS ARTICULATION OFFERS A MORE DIRECT ARTICULATION/ TRANSFER. . . . HE IS ALREADY VERY FAR AHEAD IN MATH AND OTHER SCIENCES THAN INTRO LEVEL." SAT SCORE: 1530.

HE WORE A DEMOLITION RANCH T-SHIRT

HE FLEW HIS DRONE FOR 11 MINUTES 52 SECONDS*

* "PER THE ELECTRONIC DATA FBI GATHERED, THE CONTROLLER HAD 13 FLIGHTS LOGGED IN IT. A 'FLIGHT' WOULD BE LOGGED INTO THE DRONE'S SYSTEM WHENEVER THE DRONE WAS ACTIVATED OR FLOWN. THE FBI NOTED THAT WHILE EIGHT FLIGHTS AND 20 UNIQUE IMAGES WERE PULLED FROM CROOKS' DRONE, NONE OF THE IMAGES WERE FROM JULY 13. CROOKS' DRONE FLIGHT ON JULY 13 WAS LOGGED AS FLIGHT #17. BEGINNING AT 3:51 PM . . ."

THE EAGLE HAS LANDED HIS MOTORCADE ARRIVES EVERYONE IS BEHIND THE 8-BALL ALREADY EVERYBODY IS BEING EYEBALLED BY THESE ALIASES & ENCRYPTED ACCOUNTS HEY AMERICANS I DON'T MAKE THE RULES THE EAGLE ATE THEM THE EAGLE EATS ENGLISH IVY ENGLISH POETRY E. COLI THE EX-WIVES OF THE EX-PRESIDENTS SIT ON THE BOARDS OF DIRECTORS AT EXXON AND ALL THE FORTUNE 500 COMPANIES THEY HAVE FOREVER AND THEY WILL AGAIN MY FRIENDS MY DEAREST DEARS THE EAGLE HAS ALREADY INSTAGRAMMED EVERYTHING EUGENICS EASTER DEI EARLY RETIREMENT EMERGENCY ROOMS EXTREME WEATHER ALERTS OUR ULTIMATE EXTINCTION MY FRIENDS MY DEARS IT'S UP TO EVERY RED-BLOODED AMERICAN TO SEE THE WHITETAIL DEER IN THE HEADLIGHTS IT'S EITHER EAT OR BE EATEN IT'S ALWAYS BEEN AND IT WILL ALWAYS BE THE AMERICAN DREAM*

---

* "AND, ONCE AGAIN, WE AIRED SOME CONCERNS ABOUT THAT BIG OPEN AREA FROM THE EASTERN APPROACH, THE TOWER, THE WOODS, THAT SIDE OF THE BUILDING ALL THROUGH UP TO THE FENCES. AND AT THAT POINT [CS TL] CS TL—AND HE SAID IT IN LIKE A THIRD PERSON THAT HE WAS INFORMED OR THEY WERE SUPPOSED TO BE PUTTING A FENCING OR CURTAIN TRANSLUCENT UP ACROSS THE FENCE. I DIDN'T CLARIFY WHICH FENCE, BUT MY IMPRESSION HOW HE'S PHRASED IT, HE WAS TOLD THAT THERE WAS GOING TO BE SOME SORT OF FENCING PUT UP."

FIREWORKS SOUNDS LIKE FIRECRACKERS IT FEELS LIKE FOREVER SINCE THE 4TH OF JULY FLAMES AFLAME CAMP FIRES FIRING RANGES FIRING SQUADS SHOTS FIRED FROM AFAR SEE THE TRUMP 2024 FUCK YOUR FEELINGS FLAG FLYING THE GADSDEN RATTLESNAKE FLAG BLUE LIVES MATTER BLACK FLIES MOSQUITOES ABUZZ SEE THE RISE AGAIN IN CHRISTOFASCISM HIS FATHER SAID HE CALLED THE POLICE HE CALLED THE FEDS HE CALLED THE FBI HE MADE 43 VISITS TO THE LOCAL GUN CLUB HIS FAMILY OWNED MORE THAN A DOZEN FIREARMS HE RAISED HIS FIST FIGHT! FIGHT! FIGHT! FIELD YARROW AND FLEABANE BY THE SIDE OF THE ROAD IT'S FOREVER FROM THE NEAREST FOREVER 21 IT'S FOREVER FROM THE NEAREST TGI FRIDAYS BUT FUCK IT AMERICA FIRST*

* "I SAID THAT THEY HAD SOME FARM EQUIPMENT THEY WERE GOING TO USE IN THAT AREA OF THE RED COMBINE TRACTOR. THEY WERE GOING TO HAVE FENCING THAT SEPARATED, YOU KNOW, THE MAIN SITE FROM NOT THE MAIN SITE. AND THEN, THEY WERE GOING TO HAVE UNIFORM POLICE OFFICERS COVERING THAT 5 O'CLOCK TO PAST THE 3 O'CLOCK, OR 2 O'CLOCK AND 1 O'CLOCK AREA. SO KIND OF THAT WHOLE RIGHT SIDE OF THE STAGE."

WE GORGED ON GHOSTS UNTIL THE GHOSTS HAD GOTTEN US FROM OUR GUTS TO OUR GIZZARDS GOTTEN US FROM GEORGIA TO THE ROCK OF GIBRALTER GHOSTS I'M KINDA GOING OUT ON A LIMB HERE SAYING GHOSTS WE'RE GOING STRAIGHT TO HELL OR WE'RE GOING STRAIGHT TO BURGER KING AGAIN LET'S GO BRANDON FLAGS NEXT TO THE DOLLAR GENERAL GIG WORK A GIG ECONOMY GLOBAL WARMING THERE ARE NO GUARANTEES LIKE IN THE GILDED AGE GOLDENROD BY THE SIDE OF THE ROAD BIG LOTS BROKEN GENERATORS ONLY GAINSAY AS SHAKESPEARE USED TO SAY WHEN SOMEONE WAS THROWING DOWN HIS GAUNTLET THESE GUYS THESE GOOD OLE BOYS ARE MAKING US RUN THE GAUNTLET AGAIN RUNNING FOR THEIR AGING KING JUST LIKE A GOOD NEIGHBOR JUST LIKE THE GOOD OLD ARMY RESERVE THE GOON SQUADS WILL BE HERE AGAIN JUST LIKE GRAVEYARD SHIFTS LIKE DOLLAR STORE GLITTER LIKE GERRYMANDERING ELECTIONS JUST LIKE IT LOOKS LIKE WHEN SOMEONE PROGRAMS GOLGOTHA ON THEIR GPS*

---

* "HE WAS WALKING AROUND THE GRASSY AREA BETWEEN AGR AND THE SECONDARY FENCE LINE, KEPT LOOKING UP, LOOKING AT THE BUILDING. ONE POINT THAT IS WHAT RAISED MY SUSPICION IS HE WAS LOOKING DIRECTLY AT THE WINDOW I WAS POSITIONED AT [. . .] HE, LIKE I SAID, HE LOOKED UP AT THE WINDOW I WAS POSITIONED AT AND KEPT LOOKING AT IT. HE WALKED DIRECTLY TOWARDS THE WINDOW AND UNDERNEATH OF IT UP AGAINST THE BUILDING TO THE POINT WHERE I COULDN'T SEE HIM. THAT MADE ME FEEL AS THOUGH HE WAS LOOKING OR COULD—WAS POTENTIALLY LOOKING AT THE WINDOW TO SEE IF THERE WAS SOMEBODY INSIDE THE BUILDING. AND WHEN HE WENT UP AGAINST THE BUILDING TO WHERE I COULDN'T LOOK DOWN ON HIM, I FOUND THAT TO BE VERY SUSPICIOUS."

HE'S REAL SCRAWNY HE'S GOT GLASSES AND LONG HAIR HE'S GOT A GUN HE'S GOT A RIFLE IN HIS WHITE HANDS IT'S COMMON AROUND HERE IN THE HINTERLANDS IT'S COMMON AROUND HERE IN THE AMERICAN HEARTLAND HEART MAGAGIRL HEART HE USED THE HVAC AIR CONDITIONING UNITS TO HOIST HIMSELF UP HE DIDN'T HESITATE HUNGER GAMES MASS HYSTERIA HENBIT BY THE SIDE OF THE ROAD HOW DID HE LEARN TO BUILD THOSE IEDS HOW DID HE LEARN HOW TO BUILD THOSE DETONATORS HE WAS 20 YEARS OLD HOMELAND SECURITY CLEARANCE SALES AT HARBOR FREIGHT ANOTHER HAMBURGER AT HARDEE'S OR HAMBURGER HELPER AT HOME HELLO KITTIES HELLO AGAIN OUR HEROES ARE AMERICAN HEROES OUR HISTORY IS HINDERED AND HIDDEN HISTORY HELLO AGAIN OUR NEW-OLD KING HELLO AGAIN OUR HUNGRY EAGLE HASHTAG HUNGARY LOVES YOU*

* "FROM THERE, I WAS ABLE TO PULL MY HANDS TO MY CHEST. AND I BEGAN TO TRY TO, HOW I DESCRIBE IT IS, LIKE, GETTING OUT OF A POOL WITH YOUR HANDS, LIKE PUSHING UP, MY HEAD IS COMING UP, AND LUCKILY FOR ME, I'M LOOKING LEFT AS THAT HAPPENS. AND THAT IS WHEN I FIRST VIEW CROOKS ON THE ROOFTOP. I SEE CROOKS FACING DOWNRANGE TOWARDS THE STAGE, BUT HIS EYES ARE BACK AT ME AS I'M COMING UP. AND I WOULD SAY, LIKE, HIS FACIAL EXPRESSIONS WAS SURPRISED. HIS EYES WERE VERY BIG, LIKE, WHAT ARE YOU DOING UP HERE?"

IT'S THE INTERNET HONESTLY
INTERSTATE DELIVERIES DHL AMAZON FEDEX UPS
INCENDIARY DEVICES & EVERYTHING
IT'S THE NIMBOSTRATUS CLOUDS ON THE HORIZON

IT'S SUCH A NICE CLEAN NEIGHBORHOOD
WHATEVER HAPPENS I CAN SEE HAPPEN FROM MY WINDOW
WHATEVER MIGHT BE ON THE HORIZON
WHATEVER MIGHT BE IN YOUR IPHONE'S BROWSING HISTORY

SEE THOSE NICE QUIET KIDS

RIDING THEIR BIKES UP AND DOWN THE SIDEWALK
RIDING THEIR BIKES AROUND THE NEIGHBORHOOD
I'M JUST SO LUCKY TO LIVE HERE
WHO WANTS SOME ICED TEA SOME ICE CREAM

I KNOW IT'S TOO EARLY
IT'S JUST WE'RE SO LUCKY
TO BE ALIVE AT A TIME LIKE THIS
WE'RE JUST SO LUCKY TO BE ALIVE*

* "AND AS I CAME UP, THAT'S WHEN HE POINTED HIS FIREARM IN MY FACE. AND AT THAT TIME, I COULD SEE, YOU KNOW, HE HAD A BOOKBAG WITH HIM, I COULD SEE MAGS. I KNEW HE HAD A LONG GUN, LIKE AN AR PLATFORM. AND AS I'M COMING UP AND HE'S GOT THE GUN POINTED AT ME, I DON'T KNOW IF I REACH FOR MY GUN, IF I SLIP, BUT ALL I KNOW FROM THAT POINT IS I'M LOOKING AT HIM, AND ALL MY WEIGHT IS ON MY, LIKE, ARMS, MY HANDS, AND I DON'T HAVE A GRIP."

JOHN DOES IN THE COUNTY JAILS

JANE DOES IN THE COUNTY MORGUES

DONALD J TRUMP RFK JR ELON MUSK

JUDGE JURY AND EXECUTIONER

JAPANESE KNOTWEED BY THE SIDE OF THE ROAD

JUST FOR THE RECORD

JURY'S STILL OUT*

* "AS YOU CAN TELL BY THE VIDEO, IT'S JUST MY FINGERTIPS . . . AND FROM THERE, I JUST START YELLING OUT TO THE GUYS THAT ARE THERE, I YELL ON THE RADIO RIGHT AWAY. I START SAYING, YOU KNOW, SOUTH END, HE'S GOT A LONG GUN, MALE ON THE ROOF. I JUST KEPT REPEATING, HE'S GOT A GUN, HE'S GOT A LONG GUN. I'M TELLING THE GUYS THAT ARE AROUND, LIKE, HE'S RIGHT UP THERE, GUNS UP, EYES UP, STILL SCREAMING ON THE RADIO."

WHO KICKS WHO OUT OF THE KOUNTRY ASK THE KANDLE-KARRYING KIDS KACKLING ABT THE KOMMUNISTS IT ISN'T THAT KOMPLEX IT'S ALL ABOUT KOMPLEXION A WHITE KOUNTRY KAPITALISM KAUKASIANS MIDDLE KLASS KOUPLES KID ROCK A KORTEGE OF CROWS KAWING & KAWING SOME KALL IT A MURDER MAYBE I WILL KALL IT A MURDER TOO*

* "'KID LEARNING [SIC] AROUND BUILDING WE ARE IN. AGR I BELIEVE IT IS. I DID SEE HIM WITH A RANGEFINDER LOOKING TOWARDS STAGE. FYI. IF YOU WANNA NOTIFY SS SNIPERS TO LOOK OUT. I LOST SIGHT OF HIM. ALSO A BIKE WITH A BACKPACK SITTING NEXT TO IT IN REAR OF BUILDING THAT WAS NOT SEEN EARLIER.' ATL BEAVER ES SNIP. ATL TESTIFIED THAT HE MEANT TO TYPE 'LURKING' INSTEAD OF 'LEARNING'."

JUST LOOK AT THE LOCKHEED MARTIN FACTORY OFF THE THRUWAY IN LIBERTY NY JUST LOOK AT THE LIVES OF THE LITTLE CAESARS DELIVERY DRIVERS IT'S ALWAYS BEEN ABOUT CAPITAL ABOUT THESE EVERLASTING LUCIFERS IT'S ALWAYS BEEN ABOUT THE LABOR THEORY OF VALUE ABOUT BLUE LIVES MATTER JUST LOOK AT ALL THE LAMB'S QUARTERS BY THE SIDE OF THE ROAD IT'S A LITTLE BIT LAMENTABLE LIKE IN THE BOOK OF LAMENTATIONS "LIKE A BEAR LYING IN WAIT LIKE A LION IN HIDING" IT'S ALWAYS BEEN ABOUT WALMART MCDONALD'S ABOUT LATE-STAGE CAPITALISM IT'S ALWAYS BEEN ABOUT OLIGARCHS IMPERIALISTS DYNASTIES & KINGS YOUR LORDSHIP AS SHAKESPEARE USED TO SAY YET SOMETIMES YOU JUST HAVE TO LAUGH MY LOVES AND SOMETIMES YOU HAVE TO BE LIVID SO LET US PRAY OUR LAMENTATIONS AT LEAST THOSE OF US WHO STILL LANGUISH HERE MAY ETERNAL REST GRANT UNTO US-OF-A OH LORD AND LET PERPETUAL LIGHT SHINE UPON US*

* "FORMER PRESIDENT TRUMP, UPON FEELING A BULLET GRAZE HIS RIGHT EAR, DROPPED TO THE STAGE AND TOOK COVER. SECRET SERVICE AGENTS IMMEDIATELY RUSHED THE STAGE TO FORM A 'LES' OVER HIM. DTD ASAIC ASAIC DTD RECALLS SEEING 'A DARK LIQUID POOLING IN FRONT OF [THE FORMER PRESIDENT]'."

MY OH MY THE MILKWEED PODS ARE AMASSING LIKE MINIMUM-WAGE JOBS THEY ARE FLARING OPEN LIKE MOLOTOV COCKTAILS LIKE ELON MUSK'S MISSIONS TO MARS MUGWORT AND MEADOW BUTTERCUP BY THE SIDE OF THE ROAD MY OH MY THE NEW MONSTERS MANUFACTURE AND MANAGE THE NEW MACHINES THE NEW MACHINES MANUFACTURE AND MANIPULATE OUR MINDS LIKE MCDONALD'S OR LIKE CHARLES MANSON MAN OH MAN IT'S A MIND FUCK MY MAN BIG MACS MCRIBS SOMEBODY WRITE MACHIAVELLI WAS HERE ON THE CEMENT ABUTMENT BELOW THE US-90 OVERPASS AT THE MASSACHUSETTS NEW YORK BORDER IT'S A MAKE ENDS MEET OR MAKE A KILLING KIND OF AMERICA IT'S MUCH ADO ABOUT NOTHING AS SHAKESPEARE USED TO SAY THAT MUST BE MUSIC TO YOUR EARS MY BRETHREN MY COMRADES JUST LIKE WHITE COUNTRY MUSIC IS TO THE EARS OF THE MAGAMERICANS*

* "UPON HEARING '[S]HOOTER DOWN, SHOOTER DOWN,' THE AGENTS BEGAN TO MOVE THE FORMER PRESIDENT OFF THE STAGE TO EVACUATE HIM FROM THE BUTLER FARM SHOW. SECRET SERVICE PROTOCOL, AS DTD ASAIC ASAIC DTD PUT IT, IS TO 'GET [THE PROTECTEE] OUT OF THERE AND NOT LET SOME GUY LIKE CROOKS DECIDE THE FUTURE FOR EVERYBODY THAT WANTS TO VOTE FOR HIM.' AGENTS ARE TRAINED TO COVER THE PROTECTEE AND MAINTAIN THE BODY BUNKER TO SHIELD FROM ANY SUBSEQUENT ATTACKS. DESPITE PROTOCOL—AND DESPITE NOT KNOWING IF ADDITIONAL THREATS REMAINED—THE FORMER PRESIDENT INSTRUCTED THE AGENTS TO 'WAIT,' STOOD, RAISED HIS FIST, AND ADDRESSED THE CROWD, YELLING 'FIGHT! FIGHT! FIGHT!'"

NOTHING PREPARED US FOR NOW NOT THE NATIONAL ANTHEMS NOR NAPALM DURING VIETNAM NOT WASHINGTON DC NOT THE WORKING LIVES OF OUR IMMIGRANT GRANDPARENTS AND GREAT-GRANDPARENTS NOTHING AND NO ONE PREPARED US FOR NIGHTS LIKE THESE NEITHER DAWNS NOR DUSKS NEITHER NOSTRADAMUS NOR THE GOTHIC CATHEDRAL OF NORTE-DAME NAY NAY SAY THE NAYSAYERS NAY NAY SAY THE ANCHORS AT FOX NEWS NOTHING PREPARED US FOR THE RETURN OF MAGAMERICAN NOSTALGIA NOT EVEN ROTARY DIAL PHONES NOT EVEN THAT ELVIS PRESLEY RECORD WHERE THE KING SINGS IT'S NOW OR NEVER NOT NEW ENGLAND ASTERS BY THE SIDE OF THE ROAD NOT EVEN FORGET-ME-NOTS ANON AS SHAKESPEARE USED TO SAY NOT THE SENIOR SENATOR FROM NORTH DAKOTA NOT EVEN MOUNT RUSHMORE ITSELF NOW NOW MY FRIENDS MY COUNTRYMEN NOW NOW MY FELLOW AMERICANS MY FREUDIAN SLIPS WE PHONED THE ANCESTORS TO ASK FOR AN ANSWER BUT NOT EVEN THE ANCESTORS KNEW HOW TO ANSWER US ABOUT WHAT WE'D GONE AND GOTTEN OURSELVES INTO NOW*

---

* "DTD ASAIC ASAIC DTD RECALLING THOSE MOMENTS, TESTIFIED THAT HE HAD NEVER TRAINED FOR A SCENARIO WHERE A PROTECTEE TRIES TO STAY IN THE FACE OF A POTENTIALLY IMMINENT THREAT. DTD ASAIC ASAIC DTD CONTINUED THAT '[U]SUALLY, AFTER THEY EXPERIENCE SOMETHING LIKE THIS, THEY WANT TO LEAVE'."

ONLY TIME TOLD THE OLD STORIES

THE FAUNA AND FLORA THOSE OCEANS AND THOSE SHORES

OXALIS OX-EYE DAISY BY THE SIDE OF THE ROAD

ONLY THE OPULENCE ONLY THE GOLD COLONIALISM OIL

OH SAY CAN YOU SEE

OCEANS OF PLASTIC SODA RINGS AN ATMOSPHERE OF BLACK HOLES

ALTOCUMULOUS CLOUDS ON THE HORIZON*

---

* "SO BASICALLY, WHAT I OBSERVED, AFTER THE SHOT WAS FIRED I GOT INTO MY RIFLE, LOOKED THROUGH THE SCOPE. AND I NOTICED THAT HE WAS HE WASN'T A HIGH—HE WASN'T—IT WASN'T LIKE A HIGH SILHOUETTE OFF THE PEAK. HE WAS JUST A LOW PROFILE ON THE PEAK WHERE I COULD BASICALLY JUST MAKE OUT, LIKE I SAID, THE TOPS OF HIS SHOULDERS AND HIS HEAD. AND I COULD SEE HIS WEAPON. WHEN I FIRED MY SHOT, HE DISAPPEARED FROM MY SIGHT. AFTER TAKING MY SHOT, I IMMEDIATELY WENT AHEAD AND PUT ANOTHER LIVE ROUND INTO THE WEAPON IF I HAD TO TAKE A FOLLOW UP SHOT. AND HE DIDN'T COME BACK . . . [WE] DIDN'T KNOW IF THAT WAS A DIVERSION, IF THERE WAS ANOTHER SHOOTER."

HE PURCHASED A 5-FT ALUMINUM LADDER AT HOME DEPOT IN BETHEL PARK PA HE COULD HAVE PURCHASED IT AT HOME DEPOT IN BUTLER PA OR ANY ACE HARDWARE IN WESTERN PA ANY HOME DEPOT OR LOWE'S IN PITTSBURGH PERHAPS OR A HARBOR FREIGHT IN THAT PART OF PA THE AR-15 THAT HAD BEEN IN HIS FATHER'S POSSESSION HE PRACTICED TARGET PRACTICE AT THE CLAIRTON SPORTSMEN'S CLUB WHICH OCCUPIES 180 ACRES OF PICTURESQUE WOODLANDS IN THE SOUTHERN HILLS NEAR PITTSBURGH ON CHRISTMAS EVE EASTER HALLOWEEN VALENTINE'S DAY 6 ACTION PISTOL BAYS 3 PISTOL RANGES *E PLURIBUS UNUM* PIGWEED AND PHLOX BY THE SIDE OF THE ROAD 16 LIGHTED TRAP FIELDS REPLACEMENT THEORY PLEA BARGAINS WHITE PRIVILEGE PURE BLOODS FOR 45-47 EVERYTHING MY PEOPLE MY TIKTOK FOLLOWERS MY FACEBOOK FRIENDS EVERYTHING ABSOLUTELY EVERYTHING IS PART AND PARCEL OF THE OMNIPRESENT PANOPTICON*

* "UPON SEEING THAT CROOKS APPEARED TO BE DECEASED, BUTLER ESU ATL BUTLER ESU OP. ATL RELAYED OVER THE RADIO, '[T]HE SHOOTER IS DOWN, HE'S DOWN HARD.' AN OPERATOR FROM WASHINGTON SWAT MOVED CROOKS' GUN, A BLACK DPMS/PANTHER ARMS SEMI-AUTOMATIC RIFLE, APPROXIMATELY TEN FEET AWAY FROM HIS BODY, AND THEN HELPED TO SECURE CROOKS' ARMS BEHIND HIS BACK WITH FLEX CUFFS."

Q PREDICATED THIS*

* "A WASHINGTON SWAT OPERATOR SEARCHED CROOKS' POCKETS AND PULLED OUT A RADIO TRANSMITTER RESEMBLING A GARAGE DOOR OPENER, RAISING SUSPICIONS THAT CROOKS POSSESSED OR PLACED AN IMPROVISED EXPLOSIVE DEVICE (IED) IN THE AREA. LAW ENFORCEMENT SUBSEQUENTLY SUMMONED A BOMB SQUAD TO ASSESS THE SITUATION. ATL BUTLER ESU OP. ATL TESTIFIED THAT ALLEGHENY COUNTY POLICE DEPARTMENT BOMB SQUAD (ALLEGHENY EOD) RESPONDED, REMOVED THE BATTERY FROM THE RADIO TRANSMITTER, AND LEFT THE ROOF."

REMEMBER TO REMEMBER THIS REMIX OF HISTORY

REMEMBER THE ALTERNATIVE TAKES

REMEMBER HE WAS A REGISTERED WHITE REPUBLICAN

REMEMBER MAR-A-LAGO TWO MONTHS LATER

REMEMBER THE REDACTED DOCUMENTS

RED WAVES

RED CLOVER BY THE SIDE OF THE ROAD

REAGAN 2.0

REMEMBER THIS DAY FOREVER

IT'S A DAY FOR THE RECORD BOOKS*

* "F.B.I. ERT PERSONNEL PHOTOGRAPHED THE SCENE AND PROCESSED IT FOR PHYSICAL EVIDENCE. EIGHT 0.223 REMINGTON/5.56MM RIFLE EXPENDED CARTRIDGE CASINGS WERE FOUND ON THE ROOF NEAR CROOKS' SHOOTING POSITION . . . THE F.B.I.'S PROCESS FOR RELEASING THE AGR COMPLEX INCLUDED CLEANING THE BIOLOGICAL MATERIAL FROM THE AGR ROOF."

SOMEWHERE THERE IS SUNSHINE AND SOMEWHERE ELSE THERE ARE THUNDERSTORMS AND FLOODS SOMEWHERE THERE IS SILENCE AND SOMEWHERE THERE IS TOO MUCH SOUND IN A COUNTRY LIKE THIS COUNTRY IN A STATE LIKE THE STATE WE'RE IN SOMEWHERE THERE ARE STRATUS CLOUDS AND SOMEWHERE THERE ARE ALTOSTRATUS CLOUDS OR EVEN STRATOCUMULOUS CLOUDS SOMEWHERE BUT MOST LIKELY EVERYWHERE THERE ARE SECURITY CAMERAS THERE IS CONSTANT SURVEILLANCE 24/7 AND SOMEWHERE THERE ARE SECRET SERVICE SNIPERS AND SWAT TEAMS WITH SILENCERS ON THEIR LONG-RANGE RIFLES SOMEWHERE THERE IS FIRE AND SOMEWHERE THERE IS I.C.E. IN A COUNTRY LIKE THIS COUNTRY IN A STATE LIKE THE STATE WE'RE IN SOMEWHERE THERE IS STINGING NETTLE BY THE SIDE OF THE ROAD SOMEWHERE THERE ARE SHELTER-IN-PLACE ORDERS AND SOMEWHERE ELSE THERE ARE STOCK OPTIONS IN A TOWN LIKE THIS TOWN IN A COUNTRYSIDE LIKE THIS COUNTRYSIDE SOMEWHERE THERE ARE STORMTROOPERS AND SOMEWHERE THE SUSPECT IS DOWN ON A STREET LIKE THIS STREET IN A COUNTRY LIKE THIS COUNTRY THE SHOOTER DIES OF A SINGLE GUNSHOT WOUND AND SOMEONE ELSE SAYS THIS IS JUST LIKE WHAT HAPPENED IN SLOVAKIA*

* "SECRET SERVICE REPRESENTATIVES EXPLAINED TO THE TASK FORCE THAT LES . IN LINE WITH THE LONG-STANDING PROTOCOL, THE SECRET SERVICE LES .

TO BE OR NOT TO BE AS SHAKESPEARE USED TO SAY

"TANSY BUTTONS" BY THE SIDE OF THE ROAD

TO BE ENTERING THIS TWILIGHT OR TO BE A TERRORIST STATE*

* "AGENTS FROM THE ATF ORDERED AN IMMEDIATE E-TRACE FOR CROOKS' RIFLE TO BE COMPLETED THROUGH THE NATIONAL TRACING CENTER. THE RESULTING E-TRACE REPORT LED BACK TO CROOKS' FATHER THROUGH HIS FEBRUARY 2013 PURCHASE OF THE RIFLE. THIS LED TO THE IDENTIFICATION OF THOMAS MATTHEW CROOKS AS THE SUSPECT . . . DURING THE INTERVIEW, CROOKS' FATHER STATED THAT HE HAD PREVIOUSLY SOLD THE RIFLE TO HIS SON FOR $500."

USA! USA!*

* "CROOKS' BLOODWORK WAS POSITIVE FOR 1.7 MCG/DL ANTIMONY, 160 MCG/DL SELENIUM, AND 5.9 MCG/DL LEAD. THE ONLY POSITIVE FINDING FROM THE HEAVY METALS PANEL WHICH WARRANTED FURTHER INVESTIGATION WAS THE CONCENTRATION OF LEAD, WHICH WAS VERIFIED BY REPEAT ANALYSIS. ACCORDING TO THE REFERENCE COMMENTS FOUND ON THE HEAVY METALS PANEL, THE 'BLOOD REFERENCE LEVEL FOR ADULTS IS LESS THAN 5 MCG/DL' PER THE CENTERS FOR DISEASE AND CONTROL. DR ALLEGHENY ME STATED THAT THE PRESENCE OF LEAD COULD POSSIBLY BE A RESULT OF THE TIME CROOKS SPENT AT THE FIRING RANGE."

THE BOOK OF REVELATION THE AMERICAN REVOLUTION THE CIVIL WAR THE VIETNAM WAR AND EVERY WAR BEFORE AND SINCE WE NEVER SURRENDER NEVER SAY DIE WHITE VIGILANTES VIKING BLOOD TUFTED VETCH BY THE SIDE OF THE ROAD VOTE LIKE YOU NEVER VOTED BEFORE*

* "THE ALLEGHENY EOD PERSONNEL LOCATED A DEVICE IN THE TRUNK OF CROOKS' VEHICLE, WHICH WAS DETERMINED TO BE A SIGNIFICANT THREAT. OTHER ITEMS DISCOVERED IN CROOKS' VEHICLE INCLUDED A BOTTLE OF CLEAR LIQUID AND AN AMMUNITION STORAGE BOX FILLED WITH A QUESTIONABLE MASS THAT HAD A RADIO RECEIVER ATTACHED TO IT. ALSO FOUND IN THE VEHICLE WAS A COMMERCIALLY-PRODUCED DRONE AND A PAIRED REMOTE CONTROL. PER THE FBI, UPON DISCOVERING THE IEDS IN CROOKS' CAR, ALLEGHENY EOD 'ROBOTICALLY DISSEMBLED THE DEVICES' AND 'DUMPED THE MATERIAL IN THE STREET.' UPON VISUALLY IDENTIFYING TWO DISTINCT MATERIALS, THEY TOOK SAMPLES OF EACH, TESTED THEM, AND THEN BURNED THE REMAINDER WITH KEROSENE FOR SAFETY. THE MASS OF THESE MATERIALS IS THEREFORE UNKNOWN."

HE WORE HUNTING OUTFITS TO SCHOOL
THEY SAY IT WAS A LITTLE WEIRD BUT WHATEVER

WIDESPREAD RUMORS
WHISTLE BLOWERS

WATERCRESS WILD PARSNIP
WHITE CLOVER BY THE SIDE OF THE ROAD

WHEN TWILIGHT COMES TO THE WENDY'S PARKING LOT
WHEN NIGHT DARKENS THE WALMART PARKING LOT

SOMEWHERE SOMEONE IS BEING SERVED WITH A SEARCH WARRANT
SOMEONE SOMEWHERE IS BEING ADMINISTERED AN I.V.

SOMEONE SOMEWHERE IS WAITING FOR THEIR WELFARE CHECK
SOMEONE SOMEWHERE IS TYPING WWG1WGA INTO THE CHAT*

---

* "[SECRET SERVICE] NEVER PHYSICALLY OR VERBALLY SAID THOSE ARE GREAT POSITIONS OR BAD POSITIONS. BUT THEY HAD US MARKED IN THEIR—THE SECRET SERVICE COUNTER-SNIPERS DOCUMENTS, THE PACKETS THAT THEY GAVE US, THEY HAD THE SPECIFIC WINDOWS MARKED OF WHERE WE WERE GOING TO BE AND THEY NEVER ONCE QUESTIONED WHY WERE YOU IN THOSE WINDOWS. SO WE HAD TO ASSUME THAT THEY WERE OKAY WITH IT, TOO, IF THEY DIDN'T QUESTION OR STATE ANY CONCERNS WITH IT."

EXACTLY
AS IT WAS EXPLAINED
IN THE PUBLIC SCHOOL TEXTBOOKS*

* EXECUTIVE SUMMARY / AGR COMPLEX / FAILURES IN EXECUTION / AUTOPSY & TOXICOLOGY REPORTS / TEXT MESSAGES / "IMPROVISED EXPLOSIVE DEVICES" / MEDICAL EXAMINER / "EXPLICIT CONCERNS" / "EXPLOITED GAPS" / "MAKING DECISIONS ON THE GROUND IS INEXPLICABLE"/ EXPLOSIVES & ORDNANCE DISPOSAL (EOD) / "WITH SOME NOTABLE EXCEPTIONS"/ "UNCLASSIFIED FORM—ANY REPORT ISSUED BY THE TASK FORCE SHALL BE ISSUED IN UNCLASSIFIED FORM BUT MAY INCLUDE A CLASSIFIED ANNEX, A LAW ENFORCEMENT-SENSITIVE ANNEX, OR BOTH."

YOU KNOW YESTERDAY WAS YESTERDAY IT ISN'T COMING BACK AGAIN YET YOU MISS THOSE WHISKEY SOURS ON THE YELLOWING PORCH THE YELLOWJACKETS BUZZING AROUND YOUR KID'S LEMONADE STAND YELLOW HAWKWEED BY THE SIDE OF THE ROAD YOU KNOW LIFE AS THEY CALL IT IS A ONE-WAY STREET AND A DEAD-END STREET TO BOOT YOU KNOW HOW THE YEARS HOW THEY GO BY IN A FLASH THE LATE SUMMER SUNLIGHT WILL BE HISTORY BY THIS HOUR IN JUST A FEW DAYS SO SAY YOUR GOODBYES TO THESE BEGINNING TO YELLOW LEAVES THAT SURROUND YOU THE GOLDEN YEARS GOLD WEDDING BANDS BECAUSE YONDER COMES MY MASTER AS SHAKESPEARE USED TO SAY YOU SEE IT IN THE YELLOW GADSDEN RATTLESNAKE FLAGS YELLOW HAZARD TAPE YELLOW HAZMAT VESTS YOU SEE IT IN THE YELLOW EYE OF A DAISY*

---

* "THE AUTOPSY REPORT DESCRIBES A SINGLE ENTRY WOUND ON THE UPPER LEFT LIP, AND A CORRESPONDING EXIT WOUND IN THE RIGHT LATERAL NECK. THE BULLET TRACK IS REPORTED AS A DOWNWARD, BACKWARD, AND RIGHTWARD DIRECTION. THE EXIT WOUND OF THE RIGHT LATERAL NECK HAS AN ADJACENT PATTERNED ABRASION, WHICH IS CONSISTENT WITH A RIFLE BUTTSTOCK ABRASION. THE AUTOPSY REPORT DESCRIBES A SINGLE RE-ENTRY AND TWO RE-EXIT WOUNDS FROM FRAGMENTS AT THE UPPER RIGHT BACK ATTRIBUTABLE TO THE SAME BULLET. THE WOUNDS ARE CONSISTENT WITH A HIGH-VELOCITY BULLET FROM A DISTANT RANGE. A SMALL COPPER-COLORED METAL BULLET JACKET FRAGMENT WAS RECOVERED FROM THE UPPER RIGHT BACK DURING THE AUTOPSY. THE F.B.I. HAS POSSESSION OF THE FRAGMENT."

ORANGE EMBLAZONED ON THE TOPS OF TREES ABOVE THE RAZORWIRE FENCES SUNFLOWERS ABLAZE IN THE SUNFLOWER-SATURATED FIELDS LIKE THE CITY IN THE BOOK OF EZEKIEL BEN-BUZI TURKEY BUZZARDS CIRCLING BETWEEN US AND THE FIRE-RED SKY AMERICAN-MADE BIOHAZARDS AMERICAN-MADE BULLDOZERS Z TANKS IN UKRAINE AMERICAN-SANCTIONED BOMBS DROPPING ALL OVER GAZA THE ADZES SHARPENED AT THE PEARLY GATES THE ZODIAC THEY SAY HAS COME FULL CIRCLE AGAIN BAZOOKA JOES AT THE BARRICADES THE DIZZYING DAZE OF ORANGE SKIES PINK SKIES BLOODRED SKIES ZEUS MY FRIENDZ DOESN'T NEED A ZIPPO TO SET THIS WORLD ABLAZE CAPITALIZM DOES THE CZARS DO CUE UP THEIR HAZY OVERZEALOUS MUZAK AGAIN DON'T LISTEN TO THEIR BUZZWORDS AT THIS OUR FINAL RENDEZVOUS JUST LISTEN MY DEARZ TO THE GOODBYE BUZZING OF THE WORKER BEES*

* "THE SECRET SERVICE'S ZERO FAIL MISSION ALLOWS NO MARGIN FOR ERROR, LET ALONE FOR THE MANY ERRORS DESCRIBED IN THIS REPORT."

FALL
(. . . AGAIN)

ABIDING TRUTH MINISTRIES AC SKINS AC/OC ACT FOR AMERICA ACT FOR AMERICA NY METRO ACT ACTIVE CLUB ADAMS COUNTY PA CHAPTER MOMS FOR LIBERTY ADVANCED WHITE SOCIETY ADVOCATES PROTECTING CHILDREN AFFIRMATIVE RIGHT ALABAMA KNIGHTS OF THE KU KLUX KLAN **an American flag** ALACHUA COUNTY FL CHAPTER MOMS FOR LIBERTY ALAMANCE COUNTY TAKING BACK ALAMANCE COUNTY NORTH CAROLINA (ACTBAC) ALAMEDA COUNTY CA CHAPTER MOMS FOR LIBERTY ALAMO MILITIA ALERTAMERICA.NEWS ALEXANDER COUNTY NC CHAPTER MOMS FOR LIBERTY ALL SCRIPTURE BAPTIST CHURCH KNOXVILLE TENNESSEE ALLEGHENY COUNTY PA CHAPTER MOMS FOR LIBERTY ALLIANCE DEFENDING FREEDOM ALLIANCE OF AMERICAN KLANS **antiphonal clouds** ALLEN COUNTY IN CHAPTER MOMS FOR LIBERTY ALT-MARKET.COM ALTERNATIVE RIGHT ALTRIGHT CORPORATION AMBASSADORS OF CHRIST AMERICAN BORDER PATROL AMERICAN CHILDREN FIRST AMERICA FIRST COMMITTEE AMERICA FIRST FOUNDATION AMERICA'S PROMISE MINISTRIES AMERICA'S REMEDY AMERICA'S SURVIVAL INC. AMERICAN CHRISTIAN DIXIE KNIGHTS OF THE KU KLUX KLAN **amber waves of grain** AMERICAN CHRISTIAN KNIGHTS OF THE KU KLUX KLAN AMERICAN COLLEGE OF PEDIATRICIANS AMERICAN COMMON LAW ACADEMY AMERICAN CONFEDERATE KNIGHTS OF THE KU KLUX KLAN **an Aldi an AutoZone** AMERICAN CONSTITUTIONAL ELITES AMERICAN DEFENSE SKINHEADS AMERICAN EAGLE PARTY AMERICAN FAMILY ASSOCIATION AMERICAN FREE PRESS AMERICAN FREEDOM ALLIANCE **an abandoned NAPA Auto Parts store** AMERICAN FREEDOM DEFENSE INITIATIVE AMERICAN FREEDOM NETWORK AMERICAN FREEDOM NEWS AMERICAN FREEDOM PARTY AMERICAN FREEDOM UNION AMERICAN FRONT AMERICAN FUTURIST AMERICAN GUARD AMERICAN IDENTITY MOVEMENT/IDENTITY EVROPA AMERICAN IMMIGRATION CONTROL FOUNDATION/AMERICANS FOR IMMIGRATION CONTROL AMERICAN MEETING GROUP AUSTIN TX AMERICAN MEETING GROUP WISCONSIN AMERICAN NATIONALIST ASSOCIATION AMERICAN NATIONALIST INITIATIVE AMERICAN NATIONALIST UNION AMERICAN NATIONALIST SOCIALIST PARTY AMERICAN NAZI PARTY AMERICAN PATRIOT BRIGADE AMERICAN PATRIOT COUNCIL AMERICAN PATRIOT PARTY AMERICAN PATRIOT VANGUARD AMERICAN PATRIOTS THREE PERCENT AMERICAN PATRIOTS USA **anytime and anywhere** AMERICAN POLICE OFFICERS ALLIANCE AMERICAN POLICY CENTER THE AMERICAN PROJECT AMERICAN REGULATORS AMERICAN RENAISSANCE/NEW CENTURY FOUNDATION AMERICAN REVOLUTION 2.0 THE AMERICAN STATES ASSEMBLY **golden arches in the American landscape** AMERICAN VANGUARD AMERICAN VIKINGS AMERICAN VIKING CLOTHING COMPANY AMERICAN VISION AMERICAN WHITE KNIGHTS OF THE KU KLUX KLAN AMERICANS FOR LEGAL IMMIGRATION (ALIPAC) AMERICANS FOR TRUTH ABOUT HOMOSEXUALITY AMERICANS HAVE HAD ENOUGH AMERIKANER ANDERSON COUNTY SC CHAPTER MOMS FOR LIBERTY **again** ANNE ARUNDEL COUNTY MD CHAPTER MOMS FOR LIBERTY ANTELOPE HILL PUBLISHING APPALACHIAN RANGERS ASSOCIATION A.R.M.E.D. RIDING CLUB ARMY OF PARENTS ARIZONA BORDER RECON ARIZONA STATE MILITIA ARKANSAS DEFENSE FORCE ARKANSAS MOMS FOR AMERICA ARKTOS MEDIA ARYANFOLK.COM ARYAN FREEDOM NETWORK ARYAN KNIGHTS OF THE INVISIBLE EMPIRE ARYAN NATIONAL ARMY ARYAN NATIONS ARYAN NATIONS CHURCH OF JESUS CHRIST CHRISTIAN ARYAN NATIONS KNIGHTS OF THE KU KLUX KLAN ARYAN NATIONS (LOUISIANA) ARYAN NATIONS SADISTIC SOULS MC/SADISTIC SOULS MOTORCYCLE CLUB ARYAN NATIONS WORLDWIDE **is just the beginning** ARYAN RENAISSANCE SOCIETY ARYAN STRIKEFORCE ARYAN TERROR BRIGADE ARYAN WEAR ASATRU FOLK ASSEMBLY ASATRU FOLK ASSEMBLY NEW YORK ASSEMBLY OF CHRISTIAN ISRAELITES ASN STUDY GUIDE & UNIVERSITY (AMERICAN STATE NATIONALS) ATLAH MEDIA NETWORK ATOMWAFFEN DIVISION / NATIONAL SOCIALIST RESISTANCE FRONT AUBURN WHITE STUDENT UNION AUDIT THE VOTE PA AVOW (ANOTHER VOICE OF WARNING) **of against** AZ ACTIVE CLUB AZ DESERT GUARDIANS AZ PATRIOTS

BIG LOTS!

BALDWIN COUNTY AL CHAPTER MOMS FOR LIBERTY BALTIMORE COUNTY MD CHAPTER MOMS FOR LIBERTY BARNES REVIEW/FOUNDATION FOR ECONOMIC LIBERTY INC. THE BASE BATTALION 14 **Bitcoin** BAY COUNTY FL CHAPTER MOMS FOR LIBERTY BAY STATE ACTIVE CLUB BE ACTIVE FRONT USA BEAUFORT COUNTY SC CHAPTER MOMS FOR LIBERTY BEAVER COUNTY PA CHAPTER MOMS FOR LIBERTY **Botox** BEDFORD COUNTY MILITIA BEDFORD COUNTY VA CHAPTER MOMS FOR LIBERTY BENTON COUNTY AR CHAPTER MOMS FOR LIBERTY BENTON COUNTY WA CHAPTER MOMS FOR LIBERTY BERGEN COUNTY HOOLIGANS BERGEN COUNTY NJ CHAPTER MOMS FOR LIBERTY BERKELEY COUNTY SC CHAPTER MOMS FOR LIBERTY BERKS COUNTY PA CHAPTER MOMS FOR LIBERTY BERKS COUNTY PATRIOTS BERNALILLO COUNTY NM CHAPTER MOMS FOR LIBERTY BEXAR COUNTY TX CHAPTER MOMS FOR LIBERTY BIBLE BELIEVERS FELLOWSHIP **another bankruptcy** BIG SKY ACTIVE CLUB BLADEN COUNTY NC CHAPTER MOMS FOR LIBERTY BLOOD & HONOUR USA BLOOD AND HONOUR SOCIAL CLUB BLOOD RIVER RADIO **burning bridges** BLOOD TRIBE BOB'S UNDERGROUND GRADUATE SEMINAR/ BUGS BOOGALOOS BOONE COUNTY KY CHAPTER MOMS FOR LIBERTY **vacant banks** BORDER NETWORK NEWS BORDERKEEPERS OF ALABAMA BOULDER COUNTY CO CHAPTER MOMS FOR LIBERTY BRANCH COUNTY MI CHAPTER MOMS FOR LIBERTY BREVARD COUNTY FL CHAPTER MOMS FOR LIBERTY BROTHERHOOD OF LIGHT RECORDINGS **bats in an abandoned Big Lots** BROWARD COUNTY FL CHAPTER MOMS FOR LIBERTY BURLINGTON COUNTY NJ CHAPTER MOMS FOR LIBERTY BUCKS COUNTY PA CHAPTER MOMS FOR LIBERTY BUNCOMBE COUNTY NC CHAPTER MOMS FOR LIBERTY

PUSH
Coca-Cola

CABARRUS COUNTY NC CHAPTER MOMS FOR LIBERTY THE CALIFORNIA ASSEMBLY CALIFORNIA BLACKSHIRTS CALIFORNIA COALITION FOR IMMIGRATION REFORM CALIFORNIA FAMILY COUNCIL CALIFORNIA SKINHEADS **cul-de-sacs** CALIFORNIA STATE MILITIA CALIFORNIANS FOR POPULATION STABILIZATION CAMP CONSTITUTION CAMP LONESTAR CAMPBELL COUNTY KY CHAPTER MOMS FOR LIBERTY CAMPUS MINISTRY USA CANADIAN COUNTY OK CHAPTER MOMS FOR LIBERTY CAPE MAY COUNTY NJ CHAPTER MOMS FOR LIBERTY CARLISLE LIGHT INFANTRY CARROLL COUNTY MD CHAPTER MOMS FOR LIBERTY CASS COUNTY IN CHAPTER MOMS FOR LIBERTY CATHOLIC FAMILY NEWS/CATHOLIC FAMILY MINISTRIES INC. CECIL COUNTY MD CHAPTER MOMS FOR LIBERTY CENTER FOR CHRISTIAN VIRTUE CENTER FOR FAMILY AND HUMAN RIGHTS (C-FAM) CENTER FOR IMMIGRATION STUDIES CENTER FOR PERPETUAL DIVERSITY **cirrocumulus clouds** CENTER FOR SELF GOVERNANCE CENTER FOR THE ADVANCEMENT OF OCCIDENTAL CULTURE CENTRAL CA ACTIVE CLUB CHALCEDON FOUNDATION CHARLESTON COUNTY SC CHAPTER MOMS FOR LIBERTY CHATHAM COUNTY NC CHAPTER MOMS FOR LIBERTY CHATTOOGA COUNTY GA CHAPTER MOMS FOR LIBERTY CHESTER COUNTY PA CHAPTER MOMS FOR LIBERTY CHILD AND PARENT RIGHTS CAMPAIGN CHRIST THE KING CHURCH LARKSPUR COLORADO CHRIST THE KING REFORMED CHURCH OF CHARLOTTE MICHIGAN CHRISTIAN AMERICAN KNIGHTS OF THE KU KLUX KLAN **“cancel culture”** CHRISTIAN AMERICAN MINISTRIES CHRISTIAN CIVIL RIGHTS WATCH CHRISTIAN DEFENSE LEAGUE CHRISTIAN EXODUS CHRISTIAN IDENTITY CHURCH ARYAN NATIONS CHRISTIAN REVIVAL CENTER CHRISTOGENEA CHURCH MILITANT / ST. MICHAEL'S MEDIA CHURCH OF ARYANITY / ORDER OF THE WESTERN KNIGHTS TEMPLAR CHURCH OF BEN KLASSEN CHURCH OF THE AMERICAN CHRISTIAN KNIGHTS CHURCH OF THE KU KLUX KLAN CHURCH OF THE NATIONAL KNIGHTS OF THE KU KLUX KLAN **cryptocurrency** CHURCH OF THE SONS OF YHVH/CHURCH OF THE SONS OF YHWH CIRCLE OF SOVEREIGNS CITIZEN REVIEW CITIZENS FOR COMMUNITY VALUES CITIZENS FOR RESPONSIBLE EDUCATION CITIZENS MILITIA OF MISSISSIPPI CITIZENS ORGANIZED TO RESTORE RIGHTS CITRUS COUNTY FL CHAPTER MOMS FOR LIBERTY CIVILIAN DEFENSE FORCE CLARK COUNTY NV CHAPTER MOMS FOR LIBERTY CLAY COUNTY FL CHAPTER MOMS FOR LIBERTY CLOCKWORK CREW THE COLCHESTER COLLECTION COLD DEAD HANDS 2ND AMENDMENT ADVOCACY GROUP COLLETON COUNTY SC CHAPTER MOMS FOR LIBERTY COLLIER COUNTY FL CHAPTER MOMS FOR LIBERTY COLLIN COUNTY TX CHAPTER MOMS FOR LIBERTY COLORADO ALLIANCE FOR IMMIGRATION REFORM COLORADO JURAL ASSEMBLY COMMITTEE FOR OPEN DEBATE ON THE HOLOCAUST CONCERNED CHRISTIAN CITIZENS CONCERNED CITIZENS AND FRIENDS OF ILLEGAL IMMIGRATION LAW ENFORCEMENT CONFEDERATE 28 CONFEDERATE 901 CONFEDERATE HAMMERSKINS CONFEDERATE PATRIOT VOTERS UNITED CONFEDERATE WHITE KNIGHTS OF THE KU KLUX KLAN **Coke Zero** CONNECTICUT PARENTS INVOLVED IN EDUCATION CONNECTING THE DOTS CONSERVATIVE CITIZENS FOUNDATION INC. CONSERVATIVE REPUBLICANS OF TEXAS CONSTITUTION CLUB HEMET CALIFORNIA CONSTITUTION PARTY CONSTITUTIONAL COALITION OF NYS CONSTITUTIONAL EDUCATION & CONSULTING/KRISANNE HALL CONSTITUTIONAL LAW GROUP CONSTITUTIONAL PARTY OF ALASKA CONSTITUTIONAL PARTY OF PENNSYLVANIA CONSTITUTIONAL RIGHTS PAC MCLEAN VIRGINIA CONSTITUTIONAL SHERIFFS AND PEACE OFFICERS ASSOCIATION CONTRA COSTA COUNTY CA CHAPTER MOMS FOR LIBERTY COOK COUNTY IL CHAPTER MOMS FOR LIBERTY CORPORATE FREEDOM GROUP CORPUS CHRISTI NUECES COUNTY TX CHAPTER MOMS FOR LIBERTY COTTONWOOD MILITIA COUNCIL FOR SOCIAL AND ECONOMIC STUDIES COUNCIL OF CONSERVATIVE CITIZENS COUNTER-CURRENTS PUBLISHING COUNTER.FUND COURAGE IS A HABIT COVENANT NATION CHURCH OF THE LORD JESUS CHRIST COVENANT PEOPLE'S MINISTRY COWBOYS MOTORCYCLE CLUB IDAHO CRAIGHEAD COUNTY AR CHAPTER MOMS FOR LIBERTY THE CREATIVITY ALLIANCE CREATIVITY MOVEMENT CREDITORS DEBTORS CONTRACTS IN COMMERCE (CDCIC) **cawing crows** CREW 38 CUMBERLAND COUNTY PA CHAPTER MOMS FOR LIBERTY CURSUS HONORUM FOUNDATION

MASTER
DRY
CLEANERS

D. JAMES KENNEDY MINISTRIES **dusk** DAILY STORMER DAKOTA COUNTY MN CHAPTER MOMS FOR LIBERTY **might be our destiny** DALLAS COUNTY IA CHAPTER MOMS FOR LIBERTY DAUPHIN COUNTY PA CHAPTER MOMS FOR LIBERTY DAVIDSON COUNTY TN CHAPTER MOMS FOR LIBERTY **depreciating values** DEFENSE DISTRIBUTED DELAWARE ADVANCED WHITE SOCIETY DELAWARE COUNTY OH CHAPTER MOMS FOR LIBERTY DELAWARE COUNTY PA CHAPTER MOMS FOR LIBERTY **our dearly departed** DEMOCRATS AGAINST U.N. AGENDA 21 DENTON COUNTY TX CHAPTER MOMS FOR LIBERTY **another Dollar Tree** DIE AUSERWAHLTEN DIVINE INTERNATIONAL CHURCH OF THE WEB DIVINE TRUTH MINISTRIES **another Dollar General** DIXIE REPUBLIC DIXIELAND NATIONALISTS DNVF RECORDS DO NO HARM DOMINION ACTIVE CLUB DORCHESTER COUNTY SC CHAPTER MOMS FOR LIBERTY **redacted dates** DOUGLAS-CHELAN COUNTY WA CHAPTER MOMS FOR LIBERTY DOUGLAS COUNTY NE CHAPTER MOMS FOR LIBERTY **detox** DUPAGE COUNTY IL CHAPTER MOMS FOR LIBERTY DUSTIN INMAN SOCIETY DUTCHESS COUNTY NY CHAPTER MOMS FOR LIBERTY **drowning in debt** DUVAL COUNTY FL CHAPTER MOMS FOR LIBERTY

We Sell It For

EAGLE FORUM EAST BATON ROUGE PARISH LA CHAPTER MOMS FOR LIBERTY **egg prices** EAST COAST KNIGHTS OF THE TRUE INVISIBLE EMPIRE EASTER TIDINGS / CAROLYN EMERICK EASTERN HAMMERSKINS EASTERN WHITE KNIGHTS OF THE KKK EDUCATE YOURSELF EDUCATION FIRST ALLIANCE EDUCATION VERITAS EINHERJAR'S HONOR WOTANSVOLK EL PASO COUNTY TX CHAPTER MOMS FOR LIBERTY 11TH HOUR REMNANT MESSENGER **e-commerce** EMBASSY OF HEAVEN EMERGENCY NON-PROFIT ASSISTING COMMUNITIES TOGETHER (ENACT) EMMET COUNTY MI CHAPTER MOMS FOR LIBERTY EMPIRE STATE STORMERS ENDANGERED SOULS RC/CREW 519 **emptiness** ERIE COUNTY NY CHAPTER MOMS FOR LIBERTY ERIE COUNTY PA CHAPTER MOMS FOR LIBERTY EURO FOLK RADIO EUROPEAN AMERICAN ACTION COALITION EUROPEAN AMERICAN EVANGELISTIC CRUSADE EUROPEAN AMERICAN FRONT EVERGREEN EXALTED KNIGHTS OF THE KU KLUX KLAN **evacuation orders** EXODUS AMERICANUS

FAMILY DOLLAR
Smart
Coupons

FAIRFIELD COUNTY CT CHAPTER MOMS FOR LIBERTY FAITH AND HERITAGE FAITH BAPTIST CHURCH & MINISTRY FAITH EDUCATION COMMERCE (FEC UNITED) FAITH2ACTION FAITHFUL WORD BAPTIST CHURCH **Five Guys vs. *prix fixe*** FAMILY ACTION COUNCIL OF TENNESSEE THE FAMILY FOUNDATION OF VIRGINIA FAMILY HOME NORTHWEST FAMILY RESEARCH COUNCIL FAMILY RESEARCH INSTITUTE FAMILY WATCH INTERNATIONAL FASCIST FORGE FATIMA CRUSADER / INTERNATIONAL FATIMA ROSARY CRUSADE FAUQUIER COUNTY VA CHAPTER MOMS FOR LIBERTY **fair-weather friends** FEDERATION FOR AMERICAN IMMIGRATION REFORM (FAIR) / IMMIGRATION REFORM LAW INSTITUTE FELLOWSHIP OF GOD'S COVENANT PEOPLE FIGHT WHITE GENOCIDE FIRM 22 FIRST PENNSYLVANIA MOUNTAIN REGIMENT FIRST STATE PATHFINDERS 1ST WEST VIRGINIA VOLUNTEER MOUNTAIN INFANTRY (1STWVVWI) FIRST WORKS BAPTIST CHURCH EL MONTE CALIFORNIA **flex plans** FITZGERALD GRIFFIN FOUNDATION FLAGLER COUNTY FL CHAPTER MOMS FOR LIBERTY FLORENCE COUNTY SC CHAPTER MOMS FOR LIBERTY FLORIDA FAMILY POLICY COUNCIL FLORIDA MILITIA FLORIDIANS FOR IMMIGRATION ENFORCEMENT FOLKS FRONT / FOLKISH RESISTANCE MOVEMENT FORD COUNTY KS CHAPTER MOMS FOR LIBERTY **Family Dollar** THE FORSAKEN MOTORCYCLE CLUB FORSYTH COUNTY NC CHAPTER MOMS FOR LIBERTY FORT BEND COUNTY TX CHAPTER MOMS FOR LIBERTY FORZA NUOVA USA THE FOUNDATION FOUNDATION FOR ADVOCATING CHRISTIAN TRUTH / ACTS 17 APOLOGETICS FOUNDATION FOR THE MARKETPLACE OF IDEAS THE FOUNDRY 14 FIRST FRANKLIN COUNTY OH CHAPTER MOMS FOR LIBERTY FRANKLIN COUNTY PA CHAPTER MOMS FOR LIBERTY FRATERNAL ORDER OF THE CROSS FREDERICK COUNTY MD CHAPTER MOMS FOR LIBERTY FREE AMERICA RALLY FREE AMERICAN FREE EDGAR STEELE **feel the feelings** FREE MISSISSIPPI FREE NORTH CAROLINA FREE PA CAPITAL AREA CHAPTER FREE PA CUMBERLAND COUNTY FREE PA FREE LEBANON / PENNSYLVANIANS FOR FREEDOM FREE PA LANCASTER COUNTY AND SOUTH END CHAPTERS FREE PA MONTGOMERY COUNTY FREE PA PERRY COUNTY FREE PA SCHUYLKILL COUNTY FREE PA YORK COUNTY FREEDOM BOUND INTERNATIONAL FREEDOM COALITION FREEDOM FIRST SOCIETY FREEDOM FROM GOVERNMENT FREEDOM LAW SCHOOL FREEDOM RISING SUN / FREEDOM RISING SON FREEDOM SCHOOL FREEDOM YELL FREESTARTR **or fake it** FRIENDSHIP ASSEMBLY OF GOD CHURCH FRONT RANGE ACTIVE CLUB THE FRONTIERSMEN FRONTLINE POLICY COUNCIL FUHRERNET FULL HAUS FULTON COUNTY GA CHAPTER MOMS FOR LIBERTY

United
We Stand

GAB GARDEN STATE 2A GRASSROOTS ORGANIZATION GARFIELD COUNTY CO CHAPTER MOMS FOR LIBERTY **GE** GARFIELD COUNTY OK CHAPTER MOMS FOR LIBERTY GASTON COUNTY NC CHAPTER MOMS FOR LIBERTY GAYS AGAINST GROOMERS GENERATIONS / GENERATIONS WITH VISION GENESEE COUNTY VOLUNTEER MILITIA GENESIS COMMUNICATIONS NETWORK GENSPECT GEORGIA KNIGHT RIDERS OF THE KU KLUX KLAN **GM** GEORGIA THREE PERCENT MARTYRS GIDEON KNOX GROUP/MT DAILY GAZETTE GILLESPIE COUNTY TX CHAPTER MOMS FOR LIBERTY GLOBAL CRUSADERS ORDER OF THE KU KLUX KLAN GOLDEN DAWN GOLDEN STATE 45/KINDRED 45 GOLDEN STATE SKINHEADS GOLDEN STATE SOLIDARITY **GRE** GORILLA LEARNING INSTITUTE GRAND TRAVERSE COUNTY MI CHAPTER MOMS FOR LIBERTY GREAT MILLSTONE GOLDEN TRIANGLE MILITIA GOOD CITIZEN MILITIA GOYFUNDME GRANITEGROK GREAT LAKES KNIGHTS OF THE KU KLUX KLAN **"golden age"** GREEN MOUNTAIN MILITIA GREENE COUNTY MO CHAPTER MOMS FOR LIBERTY GREENE COUNTY NY CHAPTER MOMS FOR LIBERTY GREENVILLE COUNTY SC CHAPTER MOMS FOR LIBERTY GUILFORD COUNTY NC CHAPTER MOMS FOR LIBERTY GUN OWNERS OF AMERICA **(ghosts)** GWINNETT COUNTY GA CHAPTER MOMS FOR LIBERTY

H. L. MENCKEN CLUB HALL COUNTY GA CHAPTER MOMS FOR LIBERTY HAMILTON COUNTY IN CHAPTER MOMS FOR LIBERTY HAMILTON COUNTY OH CHAPTER MOMS FOR LIBERTY HAMILTON COUNTY TN CHAPTER MOMS FOR LIBERTY HAMMERSKINS **honeybees** HARFORD COUNTY MD CHAPTER MOMS FOR LIBERTY HARTFORD COUNTY CT CHAPTER MOMS FOR LIBERTY HATE CRIME STREETWEAR PRODUCTIONS THE HATED HATED AND PROUD SKINS **in the hereafter** HEALTHY AMERICAN HEATHENS MOTORCYCLE CLUB HEARTLAND DEFENDERS HEARTLAND PATRIOTS H8 PROPAGAND ART HEIRS TO THE CONFEDERACY HELP RESCUE OUR CHILDREN HELP SAVE MARYLAND HENRY COUNTY IL CHAPTER MOMS FOR LIBERTY HERITAGE AND DESTINY HERNANDO COUNTY FL CHAPTER MOMS FOR LIBERTY HETEROSEXUALS ORGANIZED FOR A MORAL ENVIRONMENT HIGHLANDS COUNTY FL CHAPTER MOMS FOR LIBERTY HILLSBOROUGH COUNTY NH CHAPTER MOMS FOR LIBERTY HILLSBOROUGH COUNTY FL CHAPTER MOMS FOR LIBERTY HISADVOCATES.ORG HOLY ORDER MINISTRY HOMELAND INSTITUTE HONOLULU HI COUNTY CHAPTER MOMS FOR LIBERTY HONORABLE SACRED KNIGHTS OF THE KU KLUX KLAN HORRY COUNTY SC CHAPTER MOMS FOR LIBERTY HOT SPRINGS COUNTY WY CHAPTER MOMS FOR LIBERTY **American history** HOWARD COUNTY IN CHAPTER MOMS FOR LIBERTY HOWARD COUNTY MD CHAPTER MOMS FOR LIBERTY HUGHES COUNTY SD CHAPTER MOMS FOR LIBERTY

IDAHO CONSTITUTIONAL SHERIFFS IDENTITY DIXIE IDENTITY NATION **incels** IDENTITY VANGUARD III% SECURITY FORCE III% UNITED PATRIOTS ILLINOIS FAMILY INSTITUTE ILLINOIS SONS OF LIBERTY **inflation** IMPERIAL KLANS OF AMERICA INCELS (ONLINE FORUM) INDIAN RIVER COUNTY FL CHAPTER MOMS FOR LIBERTY INDIANA ACTIVE CLUB **I.C.E.** INDIANA CITIZENS VOLUNTEER MILITIA INFOWARS INJEKT DIVISION INSTITUTE ON THE CONSTITUTION AKA THE AMERICAN VIEW INTERNATIONAL CONSERVATIVE MOVEMENT **"in just a couple of years . . ."** INTERNATIONAL KEYSTONE KNIGHTS OF THE KU KLUX KLAN IREDELL COUNTY NC CHAPTER MOMS FOR LIBERTY IRON CITY CRU (CITIZENS RESPONSE UNIT) IRON YOUTH **is like infinity** IRREGULARS OF OHIO RESERVE MILITIA ISABELLA COUNTY MI CHAPTER MOMS FOR LIBERTY ISD RECORDS / NS88 VIDEO

JACKSON
COUNTY
MO
CHAPTER
MOMS
FOR
LIBERTY
Jehovah's
Witnesses
JEFFERSON
COUNTY
KY
CHAPTER
MOMS
FOR
LIBERTY
junkyards
JEREMIAH
FILMS
Jeep
Cherokees
JOHN
BIRCH
SOCIETY
Dow
Jones
Industrial
Average
JOHNSON
COUNTY
KS CHAPTER
MOMS
FOR
LIBERTY
yellowjackets
JOHNSTON
COUNTY
NC
CHAPTER
MOMS
FOR LIBERTY
jackals

KANAWHA COUNTY WV CHAPTER MOMS FOR LIBERTY KAROLINA KNIGHTS OF THE KU KLUX KLAN **kaleidoscopic leaves** KENNEBEC COUNTY ME CHAPTER MOMS FOR LIBERTY KENOSHA COUNTY WI CHAPTER MOMS FOR LIBERTY KENT COUNTY MD CHAPTER MOMS FOR LIBERTY **Kwik Fill** KENT COUNTY MI CHAPTER MOMS FOR LIBERTY KERSHAW COUNTY SC CHAPTER MOMS FOR LIBERTY KEYSTONE STATE SKINHEADS KEYSTONE UNITED **kerosene** KING COUNTY WA CHAPTER MOMS FOR LIBERTY KINGDOM IDENTITY MINISTRIES KINGDOM TREASURE MINISTRIES **KitchenAid** KINIST INSTITUTE KINSMAN REDEEMER MINISTRIES KITSAP COUNTY WA CHAPTER MOMS FOR LIBERTY **Kleenex** KKK RADIO KNIGHTS OF THE HOLY IDENTITY KNIGHTS OF THE KU KLUX KLAN/CHRISTIAN REVIVAL CENTER KNIGHTS OF THE WHITE DISCIPLES KNIGHTS PARTY VETERANS LEAGUE KOSCHERTIFIED **cops in Kevlar vests** KU KLOS KNIGHTS OF THE KU KLUX KLAN

FOR
LEASE
358-8923
OPEN

LA PORTE COUNTY IN CHAPTER MOMS FOR LIBERTY LACKAWANNA COUNTY PA CHAPTER MOMS FOR LIBERTY LAKE COUNTY CA CHAPTER MOMS FOR LIBERTY LAKE COUNTY OH CHAPTER MOMS FOR LIBERTY LANCASTER COUNTY PA CHAPTER MOMS FOR LIBERTY LANCASTER COUNTY SC CHAPTER MOMS FOR LIBERTY LARAMIE COUNTY WY CHAPTER MOMS FOR LIBERTY **foreclosures** LAST MILITIA LAST SONS OF LIBERTY LAURENS COUNTY GA CHAPTER MOMS FOR LIBERTY LEAGUE OF THE SOUTH LEE COUNTY AR CHAPTER MOMS FOR LIBERTY LEGAL IMMIGRANTS FOR AMERICA LEON COUNTY FL CHAPTER MOMS FOR LIBERTY LEWIS COUNTY WA CHAPTER MOMS FOR LIBERTY LEWROCKWELL.COM LEXINGTON COUNTY SC CHAPTER MOMS FOR LIBERTY LIBERTY BAPTIST CHURCH ROCK FALLS ILLINOIS LIBERTY COUNSEL LIBERTY FIRST UNIVERSITY LIBERTY HANGOUT LIBERTY NEWS NETWORK LIBERTY ROUNDTABLE LIBERTY UNDER FIRE LIFE FORCE NETWORK **for lease** LIGHT FOOT MILITIA OF KOOTENAI COUNTY IDAHO LIGHT FOOT MILITIA 63RD BATTALION LION OF JUDAH/ JESHURUN LIONS LIVIN' THE LEGACY LIVINGSTON COUNTY MI CHAPTER MOMS FOR LIBERTY LINN COUNTY IA CHAPTER MOMS FOR LIBERTY LITCHFIELD COUNTY CT CHAPTER MOMS FOR LIBERTY LONE STAR UNITED LONG ISLAND LOUD MAJORITY **liquidation sales** LONG ISLAND MUTUAL ASSISTANCE GROUP LONOKE COUNTY AR CHAPTER MOMS FOR LIBERTY LOS ANGELES COUNTY CHAPTER MOMS FOR LIBERTY LOUDOUN COUNTY VA CHAPTER MOMS FOR LIBERTY LOUISIANA FAMILY FORUM LOVING LIBERTY NETWORK **assisted living** LOYAL WHITE KNIGHTS OF THE KU KLUX KLAN LUBBOCK COUNTY TX CHAPTER MOMS FOR LIBERTY

Main
Metro Market
GROCERIES & DELI
GROCERY
PRODUCE
SNACKS
SUBS
CHICKEN
PIZZA
EAT IN &
TAKE OUT
METRO
CLOTHING

MACOMB COUNTY MI CHAPTER MOMS FOR LIBERTY MADISON COUNTY AL CHAPTER MOMS FOR LIBERTY MADISON COUNTY MS CHAPTER MOMS FOR LIBERTY **Main Street** MADISON COUNTY OH CHAPTER MOMS FOR LIBERTY MADISON'S MILITIA MAINE MILITIA MAINE PARENTS INVOLVED IN EDUCATION MAINE MILITIA MAINE VOLUNTEER RESPONDERS MARY NOEL KERSHAW FOUNDATION MALEVOLENT FREEDOM MAMALITIA MANNERBUND **McDonald's** MARATHON COUNTY WI CHAPTER MOMS FOR LIBERTY MARCH TO EXODUS THE MARCHING PATRIOTS MARICOPA COUNTY AZ CHAPTER MOMS FOR LIBERTY MARTIN COUNTY FL CHAPTER MOMS FOR LIBERTY MARYLAND NATIONAL SOCIALIST PARTY MARYLAND STATE SKINHEADS MASS RESISTANCE **multinational corps (cops)** MASSACHUSETTS FAMILY INSTITUTE MATANUSKA-SUSITNA BOROUGH AK CHAPTER MOMS FOR LIBERTY THE MAULITIA MOTORCYCLE CLUB MAYHEM SOLUTIONS GROUP MCKEAN COUNTY PA CHAPTER MOMS FOR LIBERTY MEADE COUNTY SD CHAPTER MOMS FOR LIBERTY **militiamen** MECKLENBURG COUNTY NC CHAPTER MOMS FOR LIBERTY MEDICAL KIDNAP MEDINA COUNTY OH CHAPTER MOMS FOR LIBERTY MELROSE PATRIOTS MESA COUNTY CO CHAPTER MOMS FOR LIBERTY MIAMI-DADE COUNTY FL CHAPTER MOMS FOR LIBERTY MICHIGAN HOME GUARD MICHIGAN LIBERTY MILITIA MICHIGAN MILITIA CORPS WOLVERINES MICHIGANDERS FOR IMMIGRATION REFORM AND ENFORCEMENT THE MICRO EFFECT MIDDLE AMERICA NEWS MIDDLESEX COUNTY MA CHAPTER MOMS FOR LIBERTY MIDLAND COUNTY MI CHAPTER MOMS FOR LIBERTY **the multitudes** MIDLAND HAMMERSKINS MILITANT KNIGHTS KU KLUX KLAN MILWAUKEE COUNTY WI CHAPTER MOMS FOR LIBERTY MINNEHAHA COUNTY SD CHAPTER MOMS FOR LIBERTY MISSION: AMERICA MISSISSIPPI WHITE KNIGHTS OF THE KU KLUX KLAN MISSOURI MILITIA MOM ARMY LAS VEGAS MOM ARMY OF NEW YORK MOMS FOR AMERICA **Mass Deportation Now** MONROE COUNTY FL CHAPTER MOMS FOR LIBERTY MONROE COUNTY MI CHAPTER MOMS FOR LIBERTY MONROE COUNTY NY CHAPTER MOMS FOR LIBERTY MONROE COUNTY PA CHAPTER MOMS FOR LIBERTY MONTANA FAMILY FOUNDATION MONTGOMERY COUNTY MD CHAPTER MOMS FOR LIBERTY MONTGOMERY COUNTY PA CHAPTER MOMS FOR LIBERTY MONTGOMERY COUNTY VA CHAPTER MOMS FOR LIBERTY MORRIS COUNTY NJ CHAPTER MOMS FOR LIBERTY **Mass Extinction Event** MOUNTAIN MINUTEMEN MSR PRODUCTIONS MY BROTHER'S THREEPERS

SPECIALTY
INSULATION
MFG. CO. INC.
1909

NASSAU COUNTY NY CHAPTER MOMS FOR LIBERTY NATIONAL ALLIANCE NATIONAL ALLIANCE REFORM AND RESTORATION GROUP NATIONAL ASSEMBLY NATIONAL ASSOCIATION FOR THE ADVANCEMENT OF AMERICA NATIONAL COALITION FOR IMMIGRATION REFORM **nationalism** NATIONAL CONSTITUTIONAL COALITION OF PATRIOTIC AMERICANS NATIONAL JUSTICE PARTY NATIONAL LIBERTY ALLIANCE NATIONAL POLICY INSTITUTE NATIONAL REFORMATION PARTY NATIONAL RIGHT NATIONAL SOCIALIST CHARITABLE COALITION/GLOBAL MINORITY INITIATIVE NATIONAL SOCIALIST CLUB (NSC-131) NATIONAL SOCIALIST FREEDOM MOVEMENT NATIONAL SOCIALIST GERMAN WORKERS PARTY NEBRASKA NATIONAL SOCIALIST LEGION NATIONAL SOCIALIST LIBERATION FRONT NATIONAL SOCIALIST MOVEMENT NATIONAL SOCIALIST ORDER NATIONAL YOUTH FRONT NATIONALIST COALITION NATIONALIST INITIATIVE NATIONALIST MOVEMENT NATIONALIST WOMEN'S FRONT NATRONA COUNTY WY CHAPTER MOMS FOR LIBERTY NATSOC FLORIDA NATURAL LAW HAWAII **is never enough** NATURAL NEWS CODY WYOMING NEW ALBION NEW CALIFORNIA STATE NEW CASTLE COUNTY DE CHAPTER MOMS FOR LIBERTY NEW CENTURY PRODUCTIONS A CONVERSATION ABOUT RACE NEW COLUMBIA MOVEMENT NEW ENGLAND MINUTEMEN NEW HANOVER COUNTY NC CHAPTER MOMS FOR LIBERTY NEW JERSEY EUROPEAN HERITAGE ASSOCIATION NEW JERSEY PARENTS INVOLVED IN EDUCATION NEW JERSEY PROJECT **narcotics** NEW ORDER NEW SONS OF LIBERTY MCLOUD OKLAHOMA NEW YORK MILITIA TM NEW YORKERS FOR IMMIGRATION CONTROL AND ENFORCEMENT (NYICE) NEWS WITH VIEWS NEXT NEWS NETWORK NEZ PERCE COUNTY ID CHAPTER MOMS FOR LIBERTY NIAGARA COUNTY NY CHAPTER MOMS FOR LIBERTY NO LEFT TURN IN EDUCATION MAINE NO LEFT TURN IN EDUCATION NEW HAMPSHIRE NO LEFT TURN IN EDUCATION RHODE ISLAND **live nudes** NO LEFT TURN IN EDUCATION SOUTH CENTRAL PA NO LEFT TURN IN EDUCATION SOUTHEASTERN PA NO LEFT TURN IN EDUCATION SOUTHWESTERN PA NOBLE BREED KINDRED NOBLE COUNTY IN CHAPTER MOMS FOR LIBERTY NO LEFT TURN IN EDUCATION CONNECTICUT NOBLE KLANS OF AMERICA NORCAL ACTIVE CLUB NORD HERRENVOLK NORDIC ORDER KNIGHTS OF THE KU KLUX KLAN NORTH CAROLINA AMERICAN REPUBLIC NORTH CAROLINIANS FOR IMMIGRATION REFORM AND ENFORCEMENT NORTH EAST OHIO WOODSMEN NORTH MISSISSIPPI WHITE KNIGHTS OF THE KU KLUX KLAN NORTH WESTERN RESEARCH INSTITUTE NORTHERN ARIZONA MILITIA NORTHERN HAMMERSKINS **necromancers** NORTHAMPTON COUNTY PA CHAPTER MOMS FOR LIBERTY NORTHUMBERLAND COUNTY PA CHAPTER MOMS FOR LIBERTY NORTHWEST FRONT NORTHWEST HAMMERSKINS/NORTHWESTERN HAMMERSKINS NORTHWEST WOMEN'S FRONT NOW THE END BEGINS NS PUBLICATIONS NSDAP

GUNS
ABELOVE
LAW, P.C.
HOCKEY
BAUER
BAUER
BAUER
ABELOVE
LAW, P.C.
ABELOVE
LAW, P.C.
ABELOVE
LAW, P.C.
ABELOVE
LAW, P.C.

OAKLAND COUNTY MI CHAPTER MOMS FOR LIBERTY OATH KEEPERS OCCUPIED FORCES HAWAII ARMY OCONEE COUNTY GA CHAPTER MOMS FOR LIBERTY OCONEE COUNTY SC CHAPTER MOMS FOR LIBERTY OLD GLORY SKINHEADS **open carry** OCCIDENTAL DISSENT OCCIDENTAL OBSERVER OCCIDENTAL QUARTERLY/ CHARLES MARTEL SOCIETY OCEAN COUNTY NJ CHAPTER MOMS FOR LIBERTY OHIO DEFENSE FORCE HOME GUARD OHIO MILITIAMEN OHIO MINUTEMEN MILITIA OHIO PATRIOTS ALLIANCE OHIO STATE REGULAR MILITIA OHIO VALLEY MINUTEMEN CITIZEN'S VOLUNTEER MILITIA OKALOOSA COUNTY FL CHAPTER MOMS FOR LIBERTY OKLAHOMA COUNTY OK CHAPTER MOMS FOR LIBERTY OKLAHOMA KNIGHTS OF THE KU KLUX KLAN **oligarchy** OLD DOMINION KNIGHTS OF THE KU KLUX KLAN OLD GLORY KNIGHTS OF THE KU KLUX KLAN OLMSTED COUNTY MN CHAPTER MOMS FOR LIBERTY ONEIDA COUNTY NY CHAPTER MOMS FOR LIBERTY ONONDAGA COUNTY NY CHAPTER MOMS FOR LIBERTY ONSLOW COUNTY NC CHAPTER MOMS FOR LIBERTY OPERATION HOMELAND ORANGE COUNTY FL CHAPTER MOMS FOR LIBERTY ORANGE COUNTY NC CHAPTER MOMS FOR LIBERTY ORANGE COUNTY NY CHAPTER MOMS FOR LIBERTY ORANGE COUNTY SKINS OREGON STATES JURAL ASSEMBLY OREGONIANS FOR IMMIGRATION REFORM **only in America** ORIGINAL KNIGHT RIDERS KNIGHTS OF THE KU KLUX KLAN ORIGINAL KNIGHTS OF AMERICA KNIGHTS OF THE KU KLUX KLAN OSCEOLA COUNTY FL CHAPTER MOMS FOR LIBERTY OTTER TAIL COUNTY MN CHAPTER MOMS FOR LIBERTY OUR FIGHT CLOTHING OUR PLACE FELLOWSHIP OUTLAW KNIGHTS OF THE KU KLUX KLAN OUTPOST OF FREEDOM OVERPASSES FOR AMERICA OZAUKEE COUNTY WI CHAPTER MOMS FOR LIBERTY

2024
TRUMP
MAKE AMERICA GREAT AGAIN
COOK ST
RAIL ROAD
CROSSING
WEIGHT LIMIT 12 TONS

PACE CONFEDERATE DEPOT PACIFIC COAST KNIGHTS OF THE KU KLUX KLAN **pipe-bombs** PACIFIC JUSTICE INSTITUTE PACIFICA FORUM PALM BEACH COUNTY FL CHAPTER MOMS FOR LIBERTY PANHANDLE PATRIOTS RIDING CLUB PARENTS ACTION LEAGUE PARENTS AGAINST CRT/PARENTS AGAINST CRITICAL RACE THEORY LLC **pistol-whippings** PARENTS DEFENDING EDUCATION PARENTS INVOLVED IN EDUCATION PARENTS' RIGHTS IN EDUCATION NEW YORK PARENTS' RIGHTS IN EDUCATION RHODE ISLAND PARENTS' RIGHTS IN EDUCATION VERMONT PARTNERS FOR ETHICAL CARE PASCO COUNTY FL CHAPTER MOMS FOR LIBERTY PASSAIC COUNTY NJ CHAPTER MOMS FOR LIBERTY **paramedics** PASS THE SALT MINISTRIES PATRIOT AMERICA PATRIOT DEPOT/THE DISCOUNT BOOK DISTRIBUTORS PATRIOT FRONT PATRIOT PARTY OF AZ PATRIOT RIGHTS IN EDUCATION PATRIOT SHIT OUTFITTERS PATRIOTIC BRIGADE KNIGHTS OF THE KU KLUX KLAN **paradigm shifts** PATRIOTIC DISSENT BOOKS PATRIOTIC FLAGS PATRIOTS AT LARGE PATRIOTS FOR AMERICA PATRIOTS FOR DELAWARE PATRIOTS FOR OHIO PENDER COUNTY NC CHAPTER MOMS FOR LIBERTY PENNINGTON COUNTY SD CHAPTER MOMS FOR LIBERTY PENNSYLVANIA ACTIVE CLUB **Palestine** PENNSYLVANIA FAMILY INSTITUTE PENNSYLVANIA HOMELAND SHIELD PENNSYLVANIA LIGHT FOOT MILITIA PENNSYLVANIA OATH KEEPERS PENNSYLVANIA PATRIOTS UNITED PENNSYLVANIA STATE MILITIA PENNSYLVANIA VOLUNTEER MILITIA PEOPLE'S BUREAU OF INVESTIGATION PEOPLE'S RIGHTS **prisons** PHALANX PHILADELPHIA COUNTY PA CHAPTER MOMS FOR LIBERTY PICKENS COUNTY SC CHAPTER MOMS FOR LIBERTY PIERCE COUNTY WA CHAPTER MOMS FOR LIBERTY **paternalism** PIKE COUNTY PA CHAPTER MOMS FOR LIBERTY PILGRIMS COVENANT CHURCH MONROE WISCONSIN PIMA COUNTY AZ CHAPTER MOMS FOR LIBERTY PIMA COUNTY AZ WATCHMEN PINELLAS COUNTY FL CHAPTER MOMS FOR LIBERTY PIONEER FUND PIONEER LITTLE EUROPE MONTANA/PIONEER LITTLE EUROPE KALISPELL MONTANA PLACER COUNTY CA CHAPTER MOMS FOR LIBERTY PLYMOUTH COUNTY MA CHAPTER MOMS FOR LIBERTY THE POLITICAL CESSPOOL **pepper spray** POLITICAL PRISONER PROJECT BOISE IDAHO POLK COUNTY FL CHAPTER MOMS FOR LIBERTY POLK COUNTY IA CHAPTER MOMS FOR LIBERTY POLK COUNTY WI CHAPTER MOMS FOR LIBERTY THE POST AND EMAIL POTTAWATOMIE COUNTY OK CHAPTER MOMS FOR LIBERTY PRAY IN JESUS NAME PROJECT PRINCE WILLIAM COUNTY VA CHAPTER MOMS FOR LIBERTY **paramilitary** PROBE MINISTRIES PROENGLISH PROPHECY CLUB RESOURCES PROTECT AMERICA NOW PROTESTANT WHITE NATIONALIST PARTY/UNCREATED LIGHT PROUD AMERICAN PATRIOTS NETWORK PROUD BOYS PROVIDENCE ROAD BAPTIST CHURCH **Project 2025** PUBLIC ADVOCATE OF THE UNITED STATES PULASKI COUNTY AR CHAPTER MOMS FOR LIBERTY PURPLE FOR PARENTS INDIANA PUTNAM COUNTY FL CHAPTER MOMS FOR LIBERTY PUTNAM COUNTY NY CHAPTER MOMS FOR LIBERTY

Q ANON
QUEENS COUNTY NY CHAPTER MOMS FOR LIBERTY

*

quiet streets isn't it quaint don't ask questions it's quicksand

HANDICAPPED
PARKING
ONLY
NO
OVERNIGHT
PARKING
VIOLATORS
TOWED AWAY
AT VEHICLE
OWNER'S
EXPENSE
1492

R. V. BEY PUBLICATIONS RACIAL NATIONALIST PARTY OF AMERICA RACINE COUNTY WI CHAPTER MOMS FOR LIBERTY RADIO JIHAD/GLOBAL PATRIOT RADIO RADIO WEHRWOLF RADIX JOURNAL RAIR FOUNDATION REAL REPUBLIC OF FLORIDA **alt-right** THE REAL THREE PERCENTERS IDAHO THE REALIST REPORT REAPERS CONSTITUTIONAL MILITIA OF OHIO REAWAKEN AMERICA TOUR REBEL BRIGADE KNIGHTS TRUE INVISIBLE EMPIRE RED ICE RED OCTOBER RED VOICE MEDIA REDOUBT NEWS REDPILL ROADSHOW REIGN OF THE HEAVENS SOCIETY REMEMBRANCE PROJECT RENAISSANCE HORIZON **AR-15s** RENEGADE BROADCASTING RENEW AMERICA REPUBLIC BROADCASTING ROUND ROCK TEXAS REPUBLIC FOR THE UNITED STATES OF AMERICA REPUBLIC OF TEXAS RESPECT WASHINGTON RESTORED ASSEMBLY OF ELOHIM REVIVAL BAPTIST CHURCH CLERMONT AND JACKSONVILLE FLORIDA REVOLT THROUGH TRADITION REVOLUTIONARY ORDER OF THE ARYAN REPUBLIC **retribution** RHODE ISLAND PARENTS INVOLVED IN EDUCATION RHODE ISLAND PATRIOTS RICHLAND COUNTY SC CHAPTER MOMS FOR LIBERTY RIDERS UNITED FOR A SOVEREIGN AMERICA CORP RIGHT BRAND CLOTHING THE RIGHT STUFF RIGHT WING RESISTANCE RIGHTEOUS ARMY RISE ABOVE MOVEMENT RIVERSIDE COUNTY CA CHAPTER MOMS FOR LIBERTY ROCKINGHAM COUNTY NH CHAPTER MOMS FOR LIBERTY ROCKY MOUNTAIN KNIGHTS OF THE KU KLUX KLAN THE ROLLING PATRIOTS **not-so-ancient ruins** RULE OF LAW RADIO AUSTIN TEXAS ROOTBOCKS RUTH INSTITUTE

ATTENTION
PROPERTY
IS UNDER
24 HOUR
SURVEILLANCE

S14/NATIONAL SOCIALIST YOUTH DETACHMENT SACRED KNIGHTS OF THE KU KLUX KLAN SACRED TRUTH PUBLISHING & MINISTRIES SACTO SKINS/SACTO SKINHEADS SADISTIC SOULS SKINHEADS SAN BERNARDINO COUNTY CA CHAPTER MOMS FOR LIBERTY **severance packages** SAN DIEGANS FOR SECURE BORDERS SAN DIEGO COUNTY CA CHAPTER MOMS FOR LIBERTY SAN JUAN COUNTY NM CHAPTER MOMS FOR LIBERTY SAN LUIS OBISPO COUNTY CA CHAPTER MOMS FOR LIBERTY SAN MATEO COUNTY CA CHAPTER MOMS FOR LIBERTY SAN PATRICIO COUNTY TX CHAPTER MOMS FOR LIBERTY SANTA BARBARA COUNTY CA CHAPTER MOMS FOR LIBERTY SANTA ROSA COUNTY FL CHAPTER MOMS FOR LIBERTY **surveillance systems** SARASOTA COUNTY FL CHAPTER MOMS FOR LIBERTY SARASOTA PATRIOTS SAVE CALIFORNIA SCHOOL OF THE WEST SCHUYLKILL COUNTY PA CHAPTER MOMS FOR LIBERTY SCOTT COUNTY MN CHAPTER MOMS FOR LIBERTY SCOTT LIVELY MINISTRIES SCOTT-TOWNSEND PUBLISHERS SCRIPTURES FOR AMERICA MINISTRIES/SCRIPTURES FOR AMERICA WORLDWIDE MINISTRIES 2ND AMENDMENT PATCHES.COM SECURE ARKANSAS SEMINOLE COUNTY FL CHAPTER MOMS FOR LIBERTY SHASTA COUNTY CA CHAPTER MOMS FOR LIBERTY SHELBY COUNTY AL CHAPTER MOMS FOR LIBERTY SHELBY COUNTY TN CHAPTER MOMS FOR LIBERTY **SWAT teams** SHERIDAN COUNTY NE CHAPTER MOMS FOR LIBERTY SHERIFF BRIGADES OF PENNSYLVANIA SHIELDWALL NETWORK SICARII 1715 SILVER BEAR CAFÉ GARLAND TEXAS SILVER SHIELD XCHANGE SLAVES OF THE IMMACULATE HEART OF MARY SNOHOMISH COUNTY WA CHAPTER MOMS FOR LIBERTY SOCAL ACTIVE CLUB SOCIAL CONTRACT PRESS SOCIETY FOR EVIDENCE-BASED GENDER MEDICINE SOLDIERS OF THE CROSS TRAINING INSTITUTE SONS & DAUGHTERS OF LIBERTY **shadows (ghosts)** SONS OF LIBERTY SURVIVAL OUTFITTERS SOUTH AFRICA PROJECT SOUTH CENTRAL PATRIOTS WASILLA ALASKA SOUTH CENTRAL PENNSYLVANIA PATRIOTS SOUTH KNOX TEN MILERS SOUTHEAST MESA CA SOUTHEAST MICHIGAN VOLUNTEER MILITIA SOUTHERN ARIZONA MILITIA SOUTHERN CULTURAL CENTER WEOGUFKA ALABAMA SOUTHERN CULTURE CENTER SOUTHERN EUROPEAN ARYANS LEAGUE ARMY SOUTHERN FUTURE SOUTHERN MOUNTAIN KNIGHTS OF THE KU KLUX KLAN SOUTHERN NATIONAL CONGRESS SOUTHERN NATIONALIST NETWORK SOUTHERN OHIO KNIGHTS OF THE KU KLUX KLAN SOUTHERN OHIO OUTDOORSMEN SOUTHERN PATRIOT SHOPPE SOUTHERN REVIVALIST SOUTHERN SONS ACTIVE CLUB SOVEREIGN FILING SOLUTIONS SOVEREIGNTY EDUCATION AND DEFENSE MINISTRY SPARTANBURG COUNTY SC CHAPTER MOMS FOR LIBERTY SPOKANE COUNTY WA CHAPTER MOMS FOR LIBERTY SPOTSYLVANIA COUNTY VA CHAPTER MOMS FOR LIBERTY **stormtroopers** ST. CHARLES COUNTY MO CHAPTER MOMS FOR LIBERTY ST. CROIX COUNTY WI CHAPTER MOMS FOR LIBERTY ST. JOHN'S COUNTY FL CHAPTER MOMS FOR LIBERTY ST. LOUIS COUNTY MN CHAPTER MOMS FOR LIBERTY ST. LOUIS COUNTY MO CHAPTER MOMS FOR LIBERTY ST. LUCIE COUNTY FL CHAPTER MOMS FOR LIBERTY STAFFORD COUNTY VA CHAPTER MOMS FOR LIBERTY STAND UP AMERICA US STANLY COUNTY NC CHAPTER MOMS FOR LIBERTY STARK COUNTY OH CHAPTER MOMS FOR LIBERTY STATE OF JEFFERSON FORMATION STATEWIDE COMMON LAW GRAND JURY STAY IN THE LIGHT STAY IN THE FIGHT STEDFAST BAPTIST CHURCH STOKES COUNTY MILITIA STORMFRONT STRAIGHT ARM MEDIA STRONG HOLD BAPTIST CHURCH NORCROSS GEORGIA SUFFOLK COUNTY NY CHAPTER MOMS FOR LIBERTY **shots fired** SUMMIT COUNTY OH CHAPTER MOMS FOR LIBERTY SUMNER COUNTY TN CHAPTER MOMS FOR LIBERTY SUNSHINE STATE NATIONALISTS SUPER HAPPY FUN AMERICA SUPREME WHITE ALLIANCE SURE FOUNDATION BAPTIST CHURCH SWEETWATER COUNTY WY CHAPTER MOMS FOR LIBERTY

TRUMP
35464-PF
Barbato
518-325-3331

TACTICAL CIVICS ALLEGHENY COUNTY PA TACTICAL CIVICS ANDROSCOGGIN COUNTY ME TACTICAL CIVICS CARBON COUNTY PA TACTICAL CIVICS CLEARFIELD COUNTY PA **terrorism** TACTICAL CIVICS NASSAU COUNTY NY TALBOT COUNTY MD CHAPTER MOMS FOR LIBERTY TAZEWELL COUNTY IL CHAPTER MOMS FOR LIBERTY TEA PARTY OF KENTUCKY **Truth Social** TEAM AMERICA POLITICAL ACTION COMMITTEE TEAM LAW TENTH AMENDMENT CENTER **tow trucks** TEUTONIC KNIGHTS OF THE KU KLUX KLAN TEXAS EAGLE FORUM TEXAS FREEDOM COALITION TEXAS KNIGHTS OF THE KU KLUX KLAN TEXAS REBEL KNIGHTS OF THE KU KLUX KLAN TEXAS THREE PERCENTERS TEXANS FOR IMMIGRATION REDUCTION AND ENFORCEMENT **what used to be called Twitter** TEXANS FOR TRUTH THIRD REICH BOOKS THIS IS TEXAS FREEDOM FORCE THOMAS ROBB MINISTRIES THREE PERCENT LIBERTY DEFENDERS THREE PERCENT OF WASHINGTON THREEPER TACTICAL TRAINING LLC TIGHTROPE RECORDS **totalitarianism?** TIMBER UNITY TINNITUS RECORDS TIPTON COUNTY IN CHAPTER MOMS FOR LIBERTY TOM BROWN MINISTRIES TRADITIONAL CONFEDERATE KNIGHTS TRADITIONAL REBEL KNIGHTS OF THE KU KLUX KLAN TRADITIONAL VALUES COALITION TRADITIONALIST AMERICAN KNIGHTS OF THE KU KLUX KLAN TRADITIONALIST WORKERS PARTY TRADITIONALIST YOUTH NETWORK TRAVERSE CITY FAMILY/TC FAMILY TRAVIS COUNTY TX CHAPTER MOMS FOR LIBERTY TRIBAL THEOCRAT TRINITY WHITE KNIGHTS OF THE KU KLUX KLAN **Taco Bell** TRUE311.COM TRUE CASCADIA TRUE INVISIBLE EMPIRE KNIGHTS/TRUE INVISIBLE EMPIRE TRADITIONALIST AMERICAN KNIGHTS OF THE KU KLUX KLAN TRUE LIGHT PENTECOST CHURCH SPARTANBURG SOUTH CAROLINA TRUE TEXAS PROJECT TRUTH IN HISTORY TRUTH RADIO **reigns of terror** TULSA COUNTY OK CHAPTER MOMS FOR LIBERTY TUOLUMNE COUNTY CA CHAPTER MOMS FOR LIBERTY 2119 BLOOD AND SOIL CREW TYR 1 SECURITY

shield

UNCLE SAM'S MISGUIDED CHILDREN UNION COUNTY PA CHAPTER MOMS FOR LIBERTY UNION OF THREE PERCENTER AMERICAN PATRIOTS UNITED DIXIE WHITE KNIGHTS OF THE KU KLUX KLAN UNITED FAMILIES INTERNATIONAL UNITED FOR A SOVEREIGN AMERICA UNITED KLAN NATION UNITED KLANS OF AMERICA UNITED NORTHERN AND SOUTHERN KNIGHTS OF THE KU KLUX KLAN UNITED PATRIOTS FOR AMERICA UNITED PATRIOTS OF AMERICA UNITED PEOPLE OF AMERICA UNITED RIOT RECORDS THE UNITED SABAEANS WORLDWIDE UNITED SKINHEAD NATION UNITED SOCIETY OF ARYAN SKINHEADS UNITED SOUTHERN SKINS UNITED STATES OF AMERICA REPUBLIC GOVERNMENT UNITED STATES JUSTICE FOUNDATION UNITED STATES CITIZEN ALARM UNITED WHITE KNIGHTS OF THE KU KLUX KLAN UNITY AND SECURITY FOR AMERICA U.S. BORDER GUARD/U.S. BORDER GUARD & BORDER RANGERS UTAH CITIZENS ALARM UTAH CONSTITUTIONAL MILITIA UTAH PATRIOTS

*

ultraMAGA : ultramilitant : ultrafascist : unAmerican

[untranslatable]

[untranslatable]

underwater mortgages

[untranslatable]

NEVER

VANDAL BROTHERS LLC **a volt of vultures** VANGUARD AMERICA WOMEN'S DIVISION VANGUARD NEWS NETWORK VDARE FOUNDATION **vampires** VERITY BAPTIST CHURCH SACRAMENTO CALIFORNIA VERMONT PARENTS INVOLVED IN EDUCATION **venture capitalists** VERMONT STATE MILITIA VETERANS ON PATROL VILAS COUNTY WI CHAPTER MOMS FOR LIBERTY **variable capital** VINLAND CLOTHING VINLAND REBELS VINLANDERS / VINLANDERS SOCIAL CLUB **vacant buildings** VINLANDIC WERWOLF DISTRIBUTION VIRGINIA BEACH VA CHAPTER MOMS FOR LIBERTY VIRGINIA KEKOAS VIRGINIA KNIGHTS **voided checks** VIRGINIA PUBLISHING COMPANY VOICE OF IDAHO VOICE OF REASON BROADCAST NETWORK **no vacancy** VOICES AGAINST TYRANNY VOLUSIA COUNTY FL CHAPTER MOMS FOR LIBERTY

WAKE COUNTY NC CHAPTER MOMS FOR LIBERTY WALTON COUNTY FLORIDA CHAPTER MOMS FOR LIBERTY **withering wetlands** WARREN COUNTY IA CHAPTER MOMS FOR LIBERTY WARREN COUNTY KY CHAPTER MOMS FOR LIBERTY WARREN COUNTY VA CHAPTER MOMS FOR LIBERTY WARLORD SKINS WARRICK COUNTY IN CHAPTER MOMS FOR LIBERTY WARRIOR'S PRIDE CLOTHING WARRIORS FOR CHRIST MOUNT JULIET TENNESSEE WASHINGTON COUNTY AR CHAPTER MOMS FOR LIBERTY WASHINGTON COUNTY PA CHAPTER MOMS FOR LIBERTY WASHINGTON COUNTY RI CHAPTER MOMS FOR LIBERTY WASHINGTON COUNTY WI CHAPTER MOMS FOR LIBERTY **a new wasteland** WASHINGTON SUMMIT PUBLISHERS WATCHMEN BIBLE STUDY GROUP WATCHMEN OF AMERICA/WATCHMEN WAYNE COUNTY MI CHAPTER MOMS FOR LIBERTY WAYNE COUNTY NY CHAPTER MOMS FOR LIBERTY WE ARE CHANGE WE THE PEOPLE FOR CONSTITUTIONAL GOVERNMENT WELD COUNTY CO CHAPTER MOMS FOR LIBERTY **white snowcaps** WEISMAN PUBLICATIONS WEREWOLF 88 WESEARCHR WEST COAST PATRIOTS WEST OHIO MINUTEMEN WESTBORO BAPTIST CHURCH TOPEKA KANSAS WESTCHESTER COUNTY NY CHAPTER MOMS FOR LIBERTY WESTERN HAMMERSKINS WESTERN OUTLANDS SUPPLY COMPANY WESTERN WHITE KNIGHTS OF THE KU KLUX KLAN WESTMORELAND COUNTY PA CHAPTER MOMS FOR LIBERTY WHAT REALLY HAPPENED **winds** WHITE ADVOCACY MOVEMENT WHITE ARYAN RESISTANCE WHITE BOY SOCIETY WHITE CAMELIA KNIGHTS OF THE KU KLUX KLAN WHITE CHRISTIAN BROTHERHOOD OF THE KU KLUX KLAN WHITE DATE WHITE DEVIL SOCIAL CLUB WHITE KNIGHTS OF TEXAS WHITE KNIGHTS OF THE KU KLUX KLAN OF AMERICA **whipping in** WHITE LIVES MATTER WHITE MAN'S MARCH WHITE NEW YORK WHITE POWER HOUR WHITE RABBIT RADIO WHITE TRASH REBEL WHITE STUDENT UNION OF TARRANT COUNTY WHITE VOICE WHITMAN COUNTY WA CHAPTER MOMS FOR LIBERTY WILD BILL FOR AMERICA WILDMAN'S CIVIL WAR SURPLUS AND HERB SHOP **anew** WILLIAM MCKINLEY INSTITUTE WILLIAMS COUNTY ND CHAPTER MOMS FOR LIBERTY WILLIAMSON COUNTY TN CHAPTER MOMS FOR LIBERTY WILLIAMSON COUNTY TX CHAPTER MOMS FOR LIBERTY WILL2RISE WILSON COUNTY NC CHAPTER MOMS FOR LIBERTY WILSON COUNTY TN CHAPTER MOMS FOR LIBERTY **woke** WINDSOR HILLS BAPTIST CHURCH WINNEBAGO COUNTY WI CHAPTER MOMS FOR LIBERTY WINTER SOLACE PRODUCTIONS WND (WORLDNETDAILY) WOLFHOOK LIFE CLOTHING WOLVERINE WATCHMEN **war** WOMEN FIGHTING FOR AMERICA WOOD COUNTY OH CHAPTER MOMS FOR LIBERTY WOOD COUNTY WI CHAPTER MOMS FOR LIBERTY WORLD CONGRESS OF FAMILIES/HOWARD CENTER FOR FAMILY RELIGION AND SOCIETY WORLD VIEW FOUNDATIONS WRIGHT COUNTY MN CHAPTER MOMS FOR LIBERTY WTM ENTERPRISES

ALABAMA KNIGHTS OF THE KU KLUX KLAN AMERICAN CHRISTIAN DIXIE KNIGHTS OF THE KU KLUX KLAN AMERICAN CHRISTIAN KNIGHTS OF THE KU KLUX KLAN AMERICAN CONFEDERATE KNIGHTS OF THE KU KLUX KLAN AMERICAN WHITE KNIGHTS OF THE KU KLUX KLAN ARYAN NATIONS KNIGHTS OF THE KU KLUX KLAN **exhume** CHRISTIAN AMERICAN KNIGHTS OF THE KU KLUX KLAN CHURCH OF THE KU KLUX KLAN CHURCH OF THE NATIONAL KNIGHTS OF THE KU KLUX KLAN CONFEDERATE WHITE KNIGHTS OF THE KU KLUX KLAN EXALTED KNIGHTS OF THE KU KLUX KLAN **the exhaustion** GEORGIA KNIGHT RIDERS OF THE KU KLUX KLAN GLOBAL CRUSADERS ORDER OF THE KU KLUX KLAN GREAT LAKES KNIGHTS OF THE KU KLUX KLAN HONORABLE SACRED KNIGHTS OF THE KU KLUX KLAN INTERNATIONAL KEYSTONE KNIGHTS OF THE KU KLUX KLAN KAROLINA KNIGHTS OF THE KU KLUX KLAN **toxicology reports** KNIGHTS OF THE KU KLUX KLAN/CHRISTIAN REVIVAL CENTER KU KLOS KNIGHTS OF THE KU KLUX KLAN LOYAL WHITE KNIGHTS OF THE KU KLUX KLAN MILITANT KNIGHTS KU KLUX KLAN MISSISSIPPI WHITE KNIGHTS OF THE KU KLUX KLAN NORDIC ORDER KNIGHTS OF THE KU KLUX KLAN NORTH MISSISSIPPI WHITE KNIGHTS OF THE KU KLUX KLAN OKLAHOMA KNIGHTS OF THE KU KLUX KLAN OLD DOMINION KNIGHTS OF THE KU KLUX KLAN **extreme weather** OLD GLORY KNIGHTS OF THE KU KLUX KLAN ORIGINAL KNIGHT RIDERS KNIGHTS OF THE KU KLUX KLAN ORIGINAL KNIGHTS OF AMERICA KNIGHTS OF THE KU KLUX KLAN OUTLAW KNIGHTS OF THE KU KLUX KLAN PACIFIC COAST KNIGHTS OF THE KU KLUX KLAN PATRIOTIC BRIGADE KNIGHTS OF THE KU KLUX KLAN ROCKY MOUNTAIN KNIGHTS OF THE KU KLUX KLAN **Pepsi Max** SACRED KNIGHTS OF THE KU KLUX KLAN SOUTHERN MOUNTAIN KNIGHTS OF THE KU KLUX KLAN SOUTHERN OHIO KNIGHTS OF THE KU KLUX KLAN TEUTONIC KNIGHTS OF THE KU KLUX KLAN TEXAS KNIGHTS OF THE KU KLUX KLAN TEXAS REBEL KNIGHTS OF THE KU KLUX KLAN TRADITIONAL REBEL KNIGHTS OF THE KU KLUX KLAN **executive orders** TRADITIONALIST AMERICAN KNIGHTS OF THE KU KLUX KLAN TRINITY WHITE KNIGHTS OF THE KU KLUX KLAN TRUE INVISIBLE EMPIRE KNIGHTS/TRUE INVISIBLE EMPIRE TRADITIONALIST AMERICAN KNIGHTS OF THE KU KLUX KLAN UNITED DIXIE WHITE KNIGHTS OF THE KU KLUX KLAN UNITED NORTHERN AND SOUTHERN KNIGHTS OF THE KU KLUX KLAN UNITED WHITE KNIGHTS OF THE KU KLUX KLAN **saw it in yr text or on X** WESTERN WHITE KNIGHTS OF THE KU KLUX KLAN WHITE CAMELIA KNIGHTS OF THE KU KLUX KLAN WHITE CHRISTIAN BROTHERHOOD OF THE KU KLUX KLAN WHITE KNIGHTS OF THE KU KLUX KLAN OF AMERICA

IM THE
REAL
VIRUS!!
JUMAD?!

goodbye factory YAKIMA COUNTY WA CHAPTER MOMS FOR LIBERTY **gig economy** YAVAPAI COUNTY AZ PREPAREDNESS TEAM **you know** YELLOWSTONE COUNTY MT CHAPTER MOMS FOR LIBERTY **you can't get away** YOLO COUNTY CA CHAPTER MOMS OR LIBERTY **your economy** YORK COUNTY PA CHAPTER MOMS FOR LIBERTY **will always be** YORK COUNTY SC CHAPTER MOMS FOR LIBERTY **your enemy**

FIRE

. . . NAZIS AMERICAN NAZI PARTY NEO-NAZIS AZ PATRIOTS CITIZENS
FOR COMMUNITY VALUES PROUD BOYZ CITIZENS FOR RESPONSIBLE
EDUCATION NAZIS CITIZENS MILITIA OF MISSISSIPPI NEO-NAZIS CITIZENS
ORGANIZED TO RESTORE RIGHTS FASCISTZ GOOD CITIZEN MILITIA NEO
FASCISTZ HETEROSEXUALS ORGANIZED FOR A MORAL ENVIRONMENT
USA PATRIOTZ **familiez, friendz (ghostz)** INDIANA CITIZENS VOLUNTEER
MILITIA NAZIS OZAUKEE COUNTY WI CHAPTER MOMZ FOR LIBERTY PROUD
BOYZ PATRIOT PARTY OF AZ NEO-NAZIS TAZEWELL COUNTY IL CHAPTER
MOMS FOR LIBERTY KU KLUX KLANZ UNITED STATES CITIZEN ALARM
NAZIS AMERICAN NAZI PARTY NEO-NAZIS AZ PATRIOTS CITIZENS FOR
COMMUNITY VALUES **the Zoom chat is open** PROUD BOYZ CITIZENS FOR
RESPONSIBLE EDUCATION NAZIS CITIZENS MILITIA OF MISSISSIPPI
NEO-NAZIS CITIZENS ORGANIZED TO RESTORE RIGHTS FASCISTZ GOOD
CITIZEN MILITIA NEO FASCISTZ HETEROSEXUALS ORGANIZED FOR
A MORAL ENVIRONMENT USA PATRIOTZ INDIANA CITIZENS VOLUNTEER
MILITIA **pleaze turn yr cameras on** NAZIS OZAUKEE COUNTY WI CHAPTER
MOMZ FOR LIBERTY PROUD BOYZ PATRIOT PARTY OF AZ NEO-NAZIS
TAZEWELL COUNTY IL CHAPTER MOMS FOR LIBERTY KU KLUX KLANZ
UNITED STATES CITIZEN ALARM NAZIS AMERICAN NAZI PARTY NEO-
NAZIS AZ PATRIOTS CITIZENS FOR COMMUNITY VALUES PROUD BOYZ
CITIZENS FOR RESPONSIBLE EDUCATION NAZIS CITIZENS MILITIA OF
MISSISSIPPI NEO-NAZIS **unmute yrselvz** CITIZENS ORGANIZED TO RESTORE
RIGHTS FASCISTZ GOOD CITIZEN MILITIA NEO FASCISTZ HETEROSEXUALS
ORGANIZED FOR A MORAL ENVIRONMENT USA PATRIOTZ INDIANA
CITIZENS VOLUNTEER MILITIA NAZIS OZAUKEE COUNTY WI CHAPTER
MOMZ FOR LIBERTY PROUD BOYZ PATRIOT PARTY OF AZ NEO-NAZIS
TAZEWELL COUNTY IL CHAPTER MOMS FOR LIBERTY KU KLUX KLANZ
UNITED STATES CITIZEN ALARM **we end this epizode** NAZIS AMERICAN
NAZI PARTY NEO-NAZIS AZ PATRIOTS CITIZENS FOR COMMUNITY VALUES
PROUD BOYZ CITIZENS FOR RESPONSIBLE EDUCATION NAZIS CITIZENS
MILITIA OF MISSISSIPPI NEO-NAZIS CITIZENS ORGANIZED TO RESTORE
RIGHTS FASCISTZ GOOD CITIZEN MILITIA NEO-FASCISTZ HETEROSEXUALS
ORGANIZED FOR A MORAL ENVIRONMENT USA PATRIOTZ INDIANA
CITIZENS VOLUNTEER MILITIA NAZIS **at a familiar horizon** OZAUKEE
COUNTY WI CHAPTER MOMZ FOR LIBERTY PROUD BOYZ PATRIOT PARTY
OF AZ NEO-NAZIS TAZEWELL COUNTY IL CHAPTER MOMS FOR LIBERTY KU
KLUX KLANZ UNITED STATES CITIZEN ALARM NAZIS AMERICAN NAZI
PARTY NEO-NAZIS ***(. . . again)*** AZ PATRIOTS CITIZENS FOR COMMUNITY
VALUES PROUD BOYZ CITIZENS FOR RESPONSIBLE EDUCATION NAZIS
CITIZENS MILITIA OF MISSISSIPPI NEO-NAZIS CITIZENS . . .

NOTES & ACKNOWLEDGEMENTS

As wild a motherfucking joint as america is
Somebody should get this shit down, otherwise no one will believe it
Get it down
Get it down on the record

—Amiri Baraka

Materials in "WINTER" are taken from multiple sources including the C-SPAN Live Feed from January 6, 2021. Grayscale text in "SPRING," except for the letter *i* where the grayscale is inverted, is from an alphabetized (by me) list of online searches made by the Buffalo shooter, published in his 186-page white nationalist manifesto (errors are verbatim from the manifesto). Footnotes in "SUMMER" are taken from the AGR website, Wikipedia, "America First Legal Releases Academic Records of Thomas Crooks, Shooter in the First Assassination Attempt Against President Trump," and, predominantly, "United States House of Representatives Task Force on the Attempted Assassination of Donald J. Trump: Final Report of Findings and Recommendations." Grayscale text in "FALL (. . . AGAIN)" is from an alphabetized (by me) list of hate groups assembled by the Southern Poverty Law Center and supplemented by other online sources. I started writing the first poems in this book while listening to the owls in the overnight/early a.m. hours during the first months of the Covid-19 lockdowns in 2020 on the New York/Massachusetts border (unceded Mohican territories) and finished it, except for slight revisions/edits, in Matane, Québec, on the southern shore of the St. Lawrence River, December 31, 2024/January 1, 2025 (unceded Mi'kma'ki and Wabanaki territories).

Thanks to the following editors, journals, and anthologies who first published these poems (sometimes in much earlier drafts/versions), here in order of acceptance: *Ludd Gang* (a project of the UK Poets Hardship Fund/Alex Marsh, Dom Hale, & Tom Crompton), Academy of American Poets' *Poem-a-Day* (Brian Teare & Jen Benka), *New York Times* (Anne Boyer), *Three Fold* (Chris Tysh), Just Buffalo Literary Center "Poem of the Week" (R. D. Pohl & the Just Buffalo staff), *Tagvverk* (Barrett White), *Action, Spectacle* (Niki Herd & Adam Day), *Cul-de-Sac of Blood* (Gina Myers & J † Johnson), *What Rough Beast?: Poems on Trump and Trumpism* (Rip Bulkeley), *Tripwire* (David Buuck), *Shearsman* (Tony Frazer), *underbelly* (Maya Marshall & Marty McConnell), *Red Door* (Pablo Saborío & Elizabeth Torres), *Winter in America (Again: Poets Respond to 2024 Election* (Katie Sarah Zale, Paul E. Nelson, allia abdullah-matta, Christy White, Gabriella Gutiérrez y Muhs, Robert Lashley, Roxi Power, & Theresa Whitehill, eds.), *Bennington Review* (Michael Dumanis), *Michigan Quarterly Review* (Khaled Mattawa), *Landfill* (Eric Benick & Nick Rossi), *Headstone Zine* (Vincent Yin), *I Witness: An Anthology of Documentary Poems* (Kwoya Fagin Maples & Erin Murphy), *The Book of Jobs: Poems about Work* (Erin Murphy), *mnemotope* (Lilou Angelrath & Réiltín Ní Aodhagáin), and *Pamenar* (Ghazal Mosadeq).

Thanks to Anti-Robot Inundation Army who used an excerpt from "FALL" in their exhibition, *Program or be programmed*, at the Contemporary Arts Center, Cincinnati (April-June, 2025).

Thanks to Patrick Durgin at Kenning Editions for publishing a digital chapbook of "WINTER" in its entirety on January 6, 2024, and keeping it available for free online across the entire United States presidential election year in 2024 and through the Trump inauguration on January 20, 2025. Special thanks as well to Jessica Wilkinson and the staff at *Rabbit: A Journal for Nonfiction Poetry* (RMIT University, Melbourne, Australia) who reprinted the entire sequence in *Rabbit*'s "Mutiny" issue (fall 2024).

Thanks to William Dow and Geoffrey Gilbert who invited me to give a keynote talk at Documentary Poetry, Popular Politics, & Activism (June 15-17, 2023) at the American University of Paris where I gave the first public presentation of earlier versions of poems collected here in "WINTER." Thanks to Pilsen Community Books (esp. Mandy Medley: Chicago, IL.), Flow Chart Foundation (esp. Jeffrey Lependorf: Hudson, NY), Bill Ayers, and Stacy Szymaszek who helped me launch the "WINTER" chapbook on January 6, 2024 (Chicago) and January 12, 2024 (Hudson).

Thanks to the staff at Coffee House Press for continuing to support and publish my writing.

"SPRING," like everything I write, is dedicated to Lisa Arrastia. We watched the news of the Buffalo massacre while in bed together on her birthday.

Special thanks to Michael Pikus, my high school English teacher and dear friend, for saving paper copies of *The Buffalo News* in the months following the events documented in "SPRING."

Thanks, kinda, to Ove and Meena, my "writing coaches" who wake me up every morning around 5:00 a.m. to feed them and start my writing/editing/revising long before anyone else in the house gets up. (Meow.)

This book is dedicated to Matki.

Coffee House Press began as a small letterpress operation in 1972 and has grown into an internationally renowned nonprofit publisher of literary fiction, essay, poetry, and other work that doesn't fit neatly into genre categories.

LITERATURE
is not the same thing as
PUBLISHING

Funder Acknowledgments

Coffee House Press is an internationally renowned independent book publisher and arts nonprofit based in Minneapolis, MN; through its literary publications, Coffee House acts as a catalyst and connector—between authors and readers, ideas and resources, creativity and community, inspiration and action.

Coffee House Press books are made possible through the generous support of grants and donations from corporations, state and federal grant programs, family foundations, and the many individuals who believe in the transformational power of literature. This activity is made possible by the voters of Minnesota through a Minnesota State Arts Board Operating Support grant, thanks to the legislative appropriation from the Arts and Cultural Heritage Fund. Coffee House also receives major operating support from the Amazon Literary Partnership, and McKnight Foundation.

Coffee House Press receives additional support from Bookmobile; Dorsey & Whitney LLP; and the Schwab Charitable Fund.

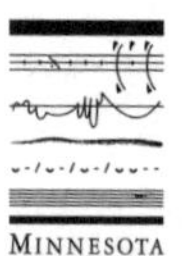

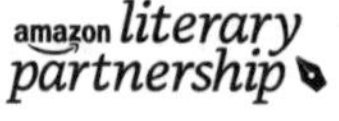

McKNIGHT FOUNDATION

The Publisher's Circle of Coffee House Press

Publisher's Circle members make significant contributions to Coffee House Press's annual giving campaign. Understanding that a strong financial base is necessary for the press to meet the challenges and opportunities that arise each year, this group plays a crucial part in the success of Coffee House's mission.

Recent Publisher's Circle members include many anonymous donors, Patricia A. Beithon, Robin Chemers Neustein, Kelli Cloutier, Theodore Cornwell, Jane Dalrymple-Hollo, Jeremy M. Davies, Mary Ebert and Paul Stembler, Kamilah Foreman, Eva Galiber, Bryan Garrett, Roger Hale and Nor Hall, William Hardacker, Randy Hartten and Ron Lotz, Carl and Heidi Horsch, Amy L. Hubbard and Geoffrey J. Kehoe Fund of the St. Paul & Minnesota Foundation, Hyde Family Charitable Fund, Kenneth & Susan Kahn, the Kenneth Koch Literary Estate, Cinda Kornblum, the Lenfestey Family Foundation, Carol and Aaron Mack, Gillian McCain, Mary and Malcolm McDermid, Daniel N. Smith III and Maureen Millea Smith, Vance Opperman, Mr. Pancks' Fund in memory of Graham Kimpton, Alan Polsky, Robin Preble, Ronald Restrepo and Candace S. Baggett, Elizabeth Schnieders, Steve Smith, Jeffrey Sugerman and Sarah Schultz, Paul Thissen, Allyson Tucker, Grant Wood, Margaret Wurtele, Aptara Inc., The Buckley Charitable Fund, and Dorsey and Whitney Foundation.

For more information about the Publisher's Circle and other ways to support Coffee House Press books, authors, and activities, please visit www.coffeehousepress.org/pages/donate or contact us at info@coffeehousepress.org.

MARK NOWAK's books include *Shut Up Shut Down, Coal Mountain Elementary, Social Poetics,* and *. . . AGAIN*, all from Coffee House Press. He has been awarded fellowships from the Guggenheim, Lannan, and Creative Capital foundations. Nowak recently wrote an introduction to Celes Tisdale's *When the Smoke Cleared: Attica Prison Poems and Journal* (Duke University Press). He is founding director of the Worker Writers School.

. . . *AGAIN* was designed by Bookmobile Design & Digital Publisher Services. Text is set in Baskerville URW and SchoolBook.